Ghost Lights of Lake Erie

By Timothy E. Harrison

Front cover image: Cleveland West Breakwater Lighthouse, Ohio
Back cover: Ashtabula, Fairpoint Harbor, Cleveland, Ohio; Black Rock, New York; and Grassy Island, Michigan.
This page: Monroe Harbor Lighthouse, Michigan

Published and copyrighted by
FogHorn Publishing, Inc.
P.O. Box 250, East Machias, Maine 04630
207-259-2121
www.FogHornPublishing.com
www.LighthouseDigest.net

Designed by Kathleen Finnegan.
Covers designed by Grace Gimena.

Printed in the United States of America
First Printing 2010

ISBN-10: 0-9778293-4-0
ISBN-13: 978-0-9778293-4-7

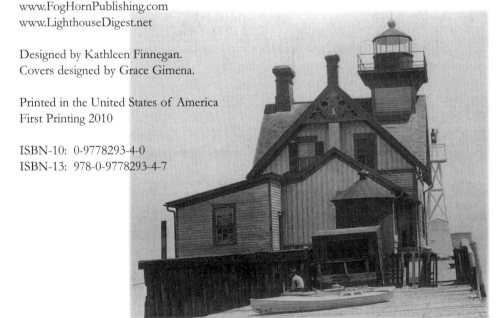

Ghost Lights of Lake Erie

Lost and Forgotten Lighthouses of a Great Lake

Dedication

Ghost Lights of Lake Erie is dedicated to the memory of
the lighthouse keepers and their family members
who served at the lighthouses on Lake Erie.
May the legacy they left us be preserved forever.

Acknowledgements

I wish to thank the United States Coast Guard, the numerous historical
societies associated with Lake Erie, Joe Foster, and Terry Pepper, who
all helped in various ways to make this book possible.

Ghosts Lights of Lake Erie

Lost and Forgotten Lighthouses of a Great Lake

Table of Contents

Ghosts Lights of Lake Erie

Lost and Forgotten Lighthouses of a Great Lake

Table of Contents

Legend of the Lighthouse

Sung to the tune of "America, the Beautiful"

Oh, beautiful, this beam of light
We see along the shore.
The lighthouse tower standing proud,
Above the ocean's roar.

Oh beacon bright, your shining light
Once guided those at sea.
The lighthouse tall protected all
Then fell to destiny.

So now, we all must keepers be,
Protect and save each one.
They are a part of history,
And tho' their work is done,

The stories told to young and old,
Will guide us come what may.
Through darkest night, To morning light,
The lighthouse shows the way!

© Jakearney 6/19/05
Words by Judi Kearney

Introduction

Lighthouses were built for one purpose only—to save lives. The fact that the people of the United States realized very early on the importance of lighthouses is what helped us to develop the best system of aids to navigation in the world. These various types of navigational aids created an elaborate means that assisted in the development of commerce allowing people and goods to arrive safely at their destinations. This, in turn, led to the rapid growth and development of the United States of America.

Realizing the importance of the lighthouses, on August 7, 1789 the First Congress of the United States of America federalized all lighthouses that had been built by the colonies. This was the first Public Works Act passed by the First Congress.

From 1789 to 1939, our nation's lighthouses operated under various government agencies and had several names: the United States Lighthouse Establishment (USLHE), The Light-House Board, The Bureau of Lighthouses, and the United States Lighthouse Service (USLHS). However, during most of its existence it was generally referred to as the "Lighthouse Service."

Proving the importance of lighthouses, the President of the United States personally appointed the early lighthouse keepers. In fact, our nation's first president, George Washington personally appointed the very first lighthouse keepers.

As well as the lighthouse keepers who most people are familiar with, the Lighthouse Service had many other employees who served in a wide variety of positions. Soon the Lighthouse Service grew into a large organization that had its own fleet of vessels, including lighthouse tenders and buoy tenders, as well as having its own manufacturing plants, supply depots, fleets of trucks, engineers, clerks, draftsmen, masons, carpenters, inspectors, engineers, machinists, clerks, and even its own police force. In fact, at one time the Lighthouse Service is believed to have had more employees decentralized outside of Washington, D.C. than any other government agency. By 1924 the United States Lighthouse Service was the largest lighthouse organization in the world.

However, modern inventions and an ever-changing government brought an end to a way of life that many of the old time lighthouse keepers could never have imagined. The first change came with electricity, followed by trains, changes in shipping routes, ocean buoys, and of course things like radar and sonar. The Lighthouse Service was slow to change and early automation came at a slow pace, mainly from public objections to removing keepers. In the 1930s some discontinued light stations were sold at auction to private owners and have remained in private ownership ever since. Rarely were they offered to the community or local nonprofits.

The biggest and most dramatic change came in 1939 when Congress, under President Franklin Roosevelt's reorganization plan, dissolved the United States Lighthouse Service and merged it into the United States Coast Guard. It was the first time in history that a military branch of the government took over a civilian agency of the government.

As automation and modern technology took hold, lighthouse keepers and many of our lighthouses were no longer needed and the Coast Guard began a long process of divesting itself of lighthouses. After automation, the Coast Guard continued to maintain some lighthouses while others were taken over by communities and nonprofits and yet others were abandoned and left to deteriorate, subject to the elements and vandalism, and some were lost.

However, it is also important to remember that in the early years, some lighthouses were simply demolished because they were old and needed to be replaced by a newer structure at the same location. Other lighthouses were demolished because they were no longer needed when an area's shipping needs changed. In many cases, especially in those early days, there might not have been a population base to support the care of a lighthouse, or it might have been in a time before people were interested in historic preservation.

There might be some facts in this book that may be questionable, but they were based on the research material at hand, some of which can be very confusing to anyone researching lighthouse history. Additionally, some research found in certain places was discovered to be incorrect and had been perpetuated and retold in other publications. However, this book is not meant to be an in-depth study of these forgotten lighthouses, how they worked or how they were built, or all the stories that are associated with them, which could fill many volumes. Instead, this book is published to help preserve for future generations the history of the United States lighthouses on Lake Erie, as well as on the Detroit River, that are no longer with us or may appear significantly different from what they once were.

Additionally, because this book is meant to be a photographic history, there are a number of lost and forgotten lighthouses that were not included, because photographs of those lighthouses either don't exist or we were unable to locate them. Among those are the Cattaraugus, Cunningham Creek, Otter Creek, Silver Creek, and Stoddard Creek lighthouses. Since this book deals only with United States Lighthouses there are also many Canadian lighthouses on Lake Erie that have been lost but are not included in this book.

Unfortunately, many of the photographs of the lighthouse keepers and the families who lived at these lighthouses have been destroyed or lost over time, while still others remain yet to be rediscovered. Locating old photographs of lighthouse keepers is a difficult and time-consuming task. Many families and descendants of the lighthouse keepers are unaware that preservationists and historians are looking for photographs, and others may not even know that they have them. However, it is more likely that many photographs and documents have been disposed of as people passed through the pages of time.

People in old photographs may have become unknown and forgotten by their descendants, and many have simply and sadly been thrown out with the trash.

However, we believe there are still many photographs and memories tucked away in attics, family Bibles, libraries and historical societies that are relevant to the lighthouses mentioned in this book, as well as other lighthouses. Hopefully this book will lead to the rediscovery of additional photographs, stories and memories that can be used in a second edition of this book or published in future editions of *Lighthouse Digest,* the lighthouse history and news magazine, so that they may be preserved for future generations.

The Buffalo Lightship

A lightship was basically a floating lighthouse that was assigned and stationed to an area where it was either too dangerous or too expensive to build a lighthouse. Because of their importance to the safety of shipping, a lightship was never allowed to leave its position, regardless of weather. When the crew's time of duty was up, a relief vessel would arrive at the location to take over its duty, so the other vessel could return to port for the shore leave of the crew and general maintenance.

Lightship duty was considered the most dangerous of all jobs in the United States Lighthouse Service and later in the U.S. Coast Guard, a statement that proved itself time and time again.

In the great storm of November 11, 1913 the *Buffalo Lightship, LV 82,* not being allowed to leave its station, sank with the loss of all six of its crewman. Only one body was ever recovered.

Eventually all lightships were replaced with modern buoys and the vessels were taken out of service. Only a handful of the lightships remain in existence with some of them now used as floating or stationary museums.

Administration of United States Lighthouses

When the first Congress of the United States federalized all lighthouses in 1792, the responsibility for them was assigned to the first Secretary of the Treasury, Alexander Hamilton.

In 1792 the day-to-day operations were assigned to the Commissioner of Revenue. During this time, the term United States Light House Establishment began being used. In 1801-2 the Secretary of the Treasury, Albert Gallatin, resumed direct control of the lighthouses.

As the Light House Establishment began to grow and become more complex, its duties were transferred back to the Commissioner of Revenue until 1820, when the nation's lighthouses became the responsibility of the 5th Auditor of the Treasury, who was Stephen Pleasonton.

Pleasonton became known as the General Superintendent of Lighthouses and for the next 32 years he personally and nearly single-handedly made every major decision regarding United States lighthouses. His immediate subordinates were the local Collectors of Custom who were given the titles of the Local Superintendent of Lights.

During Pleasonton's career, he relied heavily on the knowledge of a man named Winslow Lewis, who, although being quite knowledgeable, had motives in lighting the lighthouses that were somewhat self-serving, relying on a lamp and reflector system which he had a vested interest in. While most of the world was installing the much more effective Fresnel lens in lighthouses, Lewis did his best to keep the old system of reflectors and lamps. Additionally, Pleasonton gave little leeway to his local superintendents. Pleasonton's methods were generally weighed towards economy rather than effectiveness and efficiency, so changes and improvements were slow.

Stephen Pleasonton served as General Superintendent of Lighthouses for an amazing 32 years.

By 1851 Pleasonton's way of running things was in serious trouble with members of Congress, who finally made the changes themselves. On October 9, 1852, Congress created a nine member Light House Board comprised of a variety of military and civilian experts to take over the management of our nation's lighthouses. Commodore William B. Shubrick, USN, became the first Chairman of the Board.

Over the years, the Light House Board accomplished much of what Congress had expected of it, and our nation's system of lighthouses and aids to navigation improved immensely. During this time, the unofficial name of United States Lighthouse Service began to creep into use. However, the Light House Board became too cumbersome with the approvals of too many people needed to make a final decision.

In 1910 Congress decided to create the Bureau of Lighthouses under the control of one person, the Commissioner of Lighthouses, who would be appointed by the President of the United States. President William Howard Taft did not have any trouble in making that decision. He chose the highly competent George R. Putnam, who Taft had worked with while he was the governor of the Philippines, which had become a protectorate of the United States after the Spanish American War.

For the next twenty five years, until his mandatory retirement, under Putnam's leadership, the United States developed a massive and highly effective system of aids to navigation, which helped immensely in the development of commerce and the rapid growth of the United States.

In 1915 the United States Life Saving Service and the United States Revenue Cutter Service were merged together to create the United States Coast Guard. During those early years, there were also discussions about merging the Lighthouse Service into the Coast Guard, but the objections, many of which were quite adamant, ended the plan, at least for a while.

In 1935, a veteran Lighthouse Service employee, Harold D. King, became the second Commissioner of Lighthouses. Unfortunately, he was also the last person to serve in that capacity.

Many members of Congress continued to believe that immense savings could be instituted if the Bureau of Lighthouses were merged into the Coast Guard. On the other hand, President Franklin D. Roosevelt, in believing that war with Japan and other for-

In 1910 George Putnam was appointed as the first Commissioner of Lighthouses of the Bureau of Lighthouses. He served until his mandatory retirement in 1935.

eign powers was inevitable, wanted to increase the military and its budgets. However, Roosevelt faced opposition from a pacifist Congress and the American people who wanted us to stay out of the conflicts that were engulfing the world. Roosevelt believed that, as well as saving money, if the Coast Guard took over the Lighthouse Service, he could request additional money from Congress for the Coast Guard, which is a military organization. Additionally all the resources of the Lighthouse Service, under Coast Guard control, could help in the defenses of the United States.

The changes came when the president signed the Presidential Reorganization Act of 1939, which abolished the Bureau of Lighthouses, more commonly known as the United States Lighthouse Service. On July 7, 1939 the United States Lighthouse Service officially went out of business. It was the only time in American history that a military branch of our government took over a civilian branch of the government.

As for the lighthouse keepers, they were given the choice of remaining on as civilian lighthouse keepers or joining the Coast Guard; they split almost evenly. The transitional period was difficult to say the least. There was a lot of animosity by many of the Lighthouse Service employees, especially with some of the old time lighthouse keepers. And, in some cases, depending on the district and the Coast Guard officer in charge of a region, some of the keepers were not treated with the respect that they felt they deserved. The animosity grew between the factions when the Coast Guard started to dispose of everything that bore the words "United States Lighthouse Service" on it. Additionally, the Lighthouse Service personnel almost unanimously felt that the Coast

Guard did not have a respect for the actual lighthouse property and the way of life that was almost inbred into the lighthouse keepers and their families. However, at the outbreak of World War II, the Coast Guard came under the control of the U.S. Navy and there were more important things to be accomplished.

As time went on, the last of the civilian keepers retired and eventually only Coast Guard personnel were stationed at lighthouses.

The Coast Guard continued to grow. In 1946 the Bureau of Navigation and Marine Inspection was also abolished and its duties were absorbed into the Coast Guard. However, the Coast Guard's ever expanding duties did not deter them in effectively managing and developing new technology to manage our nation's waterways for the safety of commercial vessels, as well as pleasure boaters.

However, the cost of maintaining historic properties was not part of the Coast Guard's mandate, but they did the best they could. However, since the actual lighthouse towers were no longer needed, all that was required was an aid to navigation, something that could be accomplished with much less cost than through means other than restoring a lighthouse tower.

Eventually the Coast Guard decided to start divesting themselves of many lighthouses and declared them as excess property. In 1996 President Clinton signed into law a bill that allowed for the creation of the Maine Lights Program, which by its conclusion in July of 1998, transferred the ownership of over two dozen lighthouses to local communities, other government entities and nonprofits.

The success of the Maine Lights Program caused Congress to pass the National Historic Lighthouse Preservation Act in 2000 to allow equal footing for non profits, other government agencies and local communities to apply for free ownership of any lighthouse being excessed. If no one applied for ownership of the lighthouse being excessed, then the lighthouse could be put up for auction to the highest bidder. However, all new owners are now required to maintain strict historic guidelines in rehabilitating and maintaining the lighthouses.

Even though the ownership of many lighthouses has been transferred from the government, the U.S. Coast Guard, in many cases, continues to maintain the light in the tower as well as most other aids to navigation in the United States.

USLHS

This was the first emblem of the United States Light House Service, which was adapted from its predecessor's name United States Light House Establishment, USLHE. Eventually the single words "Light" and "House" were combined into one word: "Lighthouse."

This was the second emblem of the United States Lighthouse Service.

This emblem was created to honor the 150th anniversary of the Lighthouse Service at various events around the country. It saw almost no use, as the Lighthouse Service was merged into the Coast Guard in 1939.

The official pennant or flag of the United States Lighthouse Service was adopted by the U.S. Light House Board on September 3, 1888. Over time, flags were also designed for the Commissioner of Lighthouses and Superintendents of Lighthouses.

In later years, the pennant of the United States Lighthouse Service was slightly redesigned, giving the lighthouse a new design. This was done as a cost saving measure, giving the lighthouse a simpler design for sewing and manufacturing.

The flag or pennant of the United States Lighthouse Service was flown from Lighthouse Tenders, on lightships and in some cases light station launch boats. It was rarely flown at the actual lighthouses.

The Lighthouse Keeper's Uniform

Although the lighthouse service was a civilian organization, in an effort to promote a sense of order and discipline, in 1883, the government prescribed uniforms to the men on the lighthouse tenders and lightships. This was followed the next year by uniform regulations for the keepers at the lighthouses. Prior to that, there were no regulations and the keepers wore whatever they wanted.

Interestingly, the government never instituted uniform regulations for female lighthouse keepers.

Over the years the regulations were slightly changed but always remained basically the same. Although the government regulations required a hat of Navy design, the keepers wore a variety of hats, although they were all of a similar design or appearence.

The letter K sewn on the jacket lapel indicated the person was the head keeper. Many of the larger lighthouse stations had more than one lighthouse keeper. To distinguish the rank of the keepers, numbers were used. The number 1 sewn on the jacket lapel indicated that the person was the 1st assistant keeper. Subsequent letters indicated other keepers in position of rank. The letter 2 would be for the 2nd assistant keeper; 3 would indicate 3rd assistant keeper, and so forth. Additionally, the letter E was worn on the uniform lapel of the District Engineer.

Although there were various designs, with some early ones being very primitive, and all of being very similar, this was the most common emblem that was affixed to the hats of light-house keepers, the keepers at Lighthouse Depots, and officers on lighthouse tenders and lightships. In some cases the letters USLHE, for United States Light House Establishment, and in later years, USLHS for United States Light House Service were sewn under the emblem. For a brief time after 1939, the letters USCG, for United States Coast Guard, appeared under the emblem. In 1941 the Coast Guard adopted the same uniform regulations that had been used for the old lighthouse service to be used by the civilian lighthouse keepers; however, enlisted keepers wore a Coast Guard military uniform.

The keeper's uniforms had brass buttons. Again, over time there were a variety of designs. When the organization was known as the United States Lighthouse Establishment, the letters USLHE were used on the buttons. This eventually evolved into USLHS for the United States Light House Service. Also, eventually, the words "Light" and House" were combined into one word. Later, the image of a lighthouse was added to the buttons.

Starting in 1912, lighthouse keepers who were commended for efficiency at each quarterly inspection were awarded the red Inspectors Efficiency Star. Keepers who received the red efficiency star for three consecutive years were then awarded the blue Inspectors Efficiency Star.

Belle Isle Lighthouse

Detroit River, Michigan

Belle Isle Lighthouse in its prime was a meticulously maintained station. In this image, the drapes on the lantern room are closed to protect the valuable Fresnel lens from the harmful rays of the sun. (Detroit News *photograph,* Lighthouse Digest *archives.*)

Since Lake Erie is primarily fed by the Detroit River, a book on the lighthouses of Lake Erie would not be complete with a chapter about the Belle Isle Lighthouse.

Belle Island was originally called Snake Island because of the large population of snakes that inhabited the five and a half square mile island. After a herd of pigs were released to quell the snake population, the island was referred to as Hog Island. However, the city fathers of Detroit were not happy with that name and it was eventually and officially renamed Belle Island, which means Beautiful Island.

Because of the many shipwrecks in the area, in 1880 the United States government purchased a one and a half acre site to build a lighthouse on 20 acres of marshland which would be filled in. The architecturally attractive sturdy red brick lighthouse station was built facing the Canadian shoreline. In those days the only way to reach the island was by boat, making construction of the lighthouse a labor intensive project.

The first keeper of the light, which was illuminated on May 15, 1882, was William Badger, who later served five miles away at the stunning Windmill Point Lighthouse, in what is now Grosse Point Park. He could never have imagined that both of these well-built and architecturally attractive lighthouses would no longer exist in the future.

Badger and his family were the only ones living on the island and they apparently enjoyed the remoteness of the life they had there. But it was not without its hardships. On one occasion, when his wife fell extremely ill, Badger had to cross the river in a rowboat with his wife, fighting ice jams in the cold weather to get to a physician.

When Badger was transferred to nearby Windmill Point Lighthouse in 1885, he was replaced by Louis Fetes, Jr., who became the keeper in 1886. Interestingly, Fetes' father Louis Fetes, Sr. was a 40-year veteran of the U.S. Lighthouse Service. Louis Fetes, Jr. arrived at the lighthouse as a single man but three years later he was married. He and his wife Mary, who also became his assistant keeper, went on to raise six children, five of

The wrought iron fence around the Belle Isle Lighthouse Station gives it a true Victorian atmosphere. The round structure was used for oil storage. (United States Coast Guard photograph, Lighthouse Digest *archives.)*

whom were born on the island. One daughter, Belle, named after the island, loved to help her father with the lighthouse chores.

Getting supplies to the island was a long drawn-out process but it never bothered the Fetes family. Supplies were obtained in Detroit, and from there they were taken on a ferryboat to the Canadian side of the border and then rowed to the dock at the lighthouse. From there the supplies were carted over a winding path through the woods to a foot bridge that crossed the marsh to the lighthouse.

The remoteness of life on the island changed for the Fetes family when, in 1889, a bridge was completed to the island. Along with a bridge came a road that was built right though the marsh. Fetes recalled later on that, on the first Sunday after the bridge opened, over 1,700 horse-drawn rigs came to the island. That was the beginning of major changes and improvements that would happen to Belle Isle because it would soon become transformed into a playground for people from Detroit, especially after the introduction of the automobile.

During the next 43 years as the keeper here he only missed one day of work, and that was to attend the funeral of his sister. Fetes never took a vacation; he said he didn't want to, saying that he lived in the best place in the world and had the best job that life could have given him. In a 1924 interview he told a reporter from the *Detroit News,* "They can have their trading and selling and working in shops and factories if they want it. That life would kill me."

However, in 1929 the United States Lighthouse Service automated Belle Isle Lighthouse and Fetes was forced to retire at the age of 67. He had hoped that the government would let him stay at the lighthouse until he was 74, but that did not happen. He died three years later.

His son, Louis Fetes, III, told a reporter at the time of his death, "Loneliness was the real cause of his death," as his widow, Mary, nodded in agreement. He continued by say-

In addition to keeping the light and fog signal in operating order, it was the responsibility of the lighthouse keeper to maintain all aspects of the property. Lighthouse keeper Louis Fetes, Jr. is on the ladder, while his wife, Mary, and one of their children look on in this 1913 photograph. (Lighthouse Digest archives.)

ing, "He missed the old place that he had known for so long, the freighters going up and down the river, the responsibility during fog and storm, and the hundreds of friends who came to visit him."

Today, no one visiting the site can see any remnants of what truly was a handsome lighthouse station, one where dedicated keepers lived surrounded by the sounds of family life while they kept the waterway safe for the mariner. In 1939 the government

This vintage post card, showing Belle Isle Lighthouse from the water, was postmarked in 1909. When the lighthouse was first built there were no trees on the island. They were all planted by the lighthouse keepers. (Lighthouse Digest *archives.*)

During his 43 year tenure at Belle Isle Lighthouse, Louis Fetes, Jr. worked under the United States Lighthouse Board when it was transferred from the Treasury Department in 1903 to the newly created Department of Commerce, and again when the Lighthouse Board was dissolved and its duties were taken over by the civilian-controlled United States Bureau of Lighthouses. During that time he also witnessed the changing of the common name of his employer from the United States Lighthouse Establishment to the United States Lighthouse Service. (Detroit News *photo,* Lighthouse Digest *archives.*)

appropriated $100,000 to build a Coast Guard Life Boat Station at the site that was to be completed by 1942. The new Coast Guard station had a 75 foot tall lookout tower, which had a much shorter life than the old lighthouse did. Although the Coast Guard Station still stands, the lookout tower was not built as well as the lighthouse had been; it leaked so badly that it was eventually torn down.

For the historians who have stated that the United States Coast Guard has destroyed more American history than any other branch of the government, they could use the Belle Isle Lighthouse as one of their examples, and point to the parking lot where the historic Belle Isle Lighthouse once stood. Instead of being one of the "Ghost Lights of the Great Lakes," it might very well have been a magnificent museum honoring those who served our nation's lighthouses for the benefit of all mankind.

In 1935 the Coast Guard used the small light, as seen here, attached to the flag pole to mark the Belle Isle site. However, as shown here in this 1937 photograph, a small beacon light was then attached to the outside railing of the lantern room walkway. Although the Fresnel lens can still be seen in the tower, it was no longer being used and served only as the emergency backup light. By this time, Belle Isle was a popular picnic and excursion area as can be seen by the built-in picnic tables across from the lighthouse grounds. (Detroit News photo, Lighthouse Digest *archives.*)

Capt. Ernest Bondy USCG, inspecting the Belle Isle Lighthouse in 1937. This was probably some type of publicity photo, since the Fresnel lens, although still operational as a back up light, was no longer in use. (Lighthouse Digest *archives.*)

This Coast Guard Life Boat Station was built at the site of the former Belle Isle Lighthouse. The modern station was no match for the lighthouse that it replaced. At some point, the look-out tower shown here was taken down; however there is still a Coast Guard Station at the site. (Lighthouse Digest *archives.*)

Ecorse Lighthouse

Ecorse, Michigan

The Ecorse Lighthouse was part of a set of range lights built in 1894 and 1895 on the west side of the Detroit River near Ecorse, Michigan. The history of the lighthouses in this area is confusing and often intermingled with other lighthouses.

The first lighthouse keeper to serve here was August 'Gus' Gramer whose colorful career is mention later in this book.

It is believed that the last lighthouse keeper to serve here was Charles D. Northrup who served until the station was discontinued in the early 1900s. Reportedly, the Bureau of Lighthouses moved the keeper's house to Tawas Point Lighthouse in Michigan where it became part of the lighthouse station's complex. However, in 2002 the United States Coast Guard demolished the structure, which was the last remaining vestige of the Ecorse Lighthouse Station.

Officially known as the Ecorse Range Lighthouse, this structure has been lost to the pages of time. (Lighthouse Digest *archives.*)

Gibraltar Lighthouse

Gibraltar, Michigan

Established in 1838 at the mouth of the Detroit River on Lake Erie, the Gibraltar Light Station had two lighthouse structures and nine keepers during its existence. When the first lighthouse had deteriorated beyond repair a new lighthouse was built and completed in early 1873.

But, the second tower had a very short existence. It was discontinued in 1879 and placed in the hands of a caretaker. Eventually the lantern room was removed and installed on the South Bass Island Lighthouse in Ohio.

The last keeper was Mary Vreeland. She took over the position upon the death of her husband in January, 1876 and served until the lighthouse was discontinued. In 1895 the property was sold at auction.

(National Archives photograph.)

Although their lighthouse is long gone, the City of Gibraltar has kept its lighthouse history alive. In 2004, as part of the design of their municipal building, the city constructed a magnificent lighthouse facsimile.

Grassy Island Lighthouses

Lower Detroit River, Ecorse, Michigan

A lighthouse was first used at this location as early as 1849. By 1896 there were four lighthouses. Two were known as the Grassy Island North Channel Rear and Front Range Lights and the other two were known as the Grassy Island South Channel Front and Rear Range Lights.

John M. Bryan was a keeper of the lighthouse from December 1884 to December 1903. Bryan was a Civil War veteran who had participated in the battles at Harper's Ferry, Fredericksburg and Gettysburg. After the Battle of Antietam he was promoted to sergeant for his "gallant and meritorious conduct." In telling of his life at the lighthouse to a local newspaper reporter he told how he had to "bachelor" it in the winter months while his wife, Mary and their children, Edward, William, Jessie and James, lived on the mainland so the kids could attend school. He said he took his isolation philosophically and found company in his dog, pipe, his own books as well as a library of 36 volumes furnished by the lighthouse agency. However, even in the winter months, he would still have to row across the river for supplies when his inventory would run low. Only once did he encounter a problem from floating ice.

After his death, while on duty on December 6, 1903, the newspapers reported that he never missed a single day of work in all his years as a lighthouse keeper. Being of a hospitable nature his table and fireside were open to friends and strangers alike in his water-surrounded home. In 1891 he was credited with saving the lives of three men whose boat had capsized. Upon his death, his son Edward took over as the lighthouse keeper. Although he had assisted his father in the past, the job must not have been for him. He resigned after being on the job only three months. He and his brother William started what would become a successful boat building business.

Eventually the Grassy Island Lighthouses were deemed as no longer useful and by the 1940s all four structures had disappeared along with most of the memories and stories associated with them, which have long ago been forgotten, lost to the dusty pages of time. The Army Corp of Engineers used Grassy Island as a disposal facility to dispose of contaminated sediments dredged primarily from the Rouge River. The island eventually became part of the Wyandotte National Wildlife Refuge and is now part of the Detroit River International Wildlife Refuge.

Built in 1849 this is the first and for a while the only Grassy Island Lighthouse. In the late 1800s it was moved and became the Grassy Island South Channel Front Range Front Lighthouse. A woman is standing by the steps. She was apparently there to tend the lighthouse. Notice all the shipping in the channel. It is unknown when the lighthouse was destroyed, but it was gone from the lighthouse records in the 1940s. (Lighthouse Digest *archives.*)

By the time this image of the Grassy Island South Channel Front Range Lighthouse was taken, shipping in the channel had changed dramatically. Only one pleasure sailing vessel is seen on what otherwise had been a busy shipping channel. Look closely and you will notice the large door on the lantern room, which was unusual for this type of structure. (Lighthouse Digest *archives.*)

The 1897 Grassy Island North Channel Range Rear Lighthouse rested on a platform about eight feet off the ground. A short stairway led to the platform and entryway door to the 51 foot tall lighthouse. Although barely visible, a lighthouse keeper stood on the upper outside deck of the lighthouse to pose while this image was being taken. (Lighthouse Digest *archives.*)

This may be the earliest known photograph of the Grassy Island South Channel Rear Range Lighthouse. At this time the lantern room was of the early "bird cage" style. (Lighthouse Digest *archives.*)

This rear view of the 1896 Grassy Island South Channel Rear Range Lighthouse. Lighthouse shows a well maintained light station that any lighthouse keeper would have been proud to serve at. Lighthouse keeper James Bryan is the man standing in the boat and his wife Mary is standing on the pier to his right. The man standing with his arms folded to the left is Ryan Northrup who was an assistant lighthouse keeper. (Photograph courtesy Bacon Memorial Library.)

A wintertime front view of the 1896 Grassy Island South Channel Rear Range Lighthouse. The dog belonged to lighthouse keeper James Bryan. (Photograph courtesy of the Bacon Memorial Library.)

Grosse Ile Lighthouses

Grosse Ile, Michigan

Four lighthouses comprised the range lights that once stood here and only one of them still stands today. Built on the lower Detroit River, near Lake Erie, the first sets of range lights were built in 1891 and three years later a second set of lights was established.

The Grosse Ile South Channel Front Range Lighthouse, established in 1891, displayed a fixed red light from its tower. When it outlived its usefulness the structure was demolished. (Lighthouse Digest *archives.*)

The Grosse Ile South Channel Rear Range Lighthouse was a 41-foot tall white tower. Sadly, it no longer stands. (Lighthouse Digest *archives.*)

The Grosse Ile North Channel Rear Range Lighthouse was established in 1894. Its unusual looking 60-foot tall tower displayed a fixed white beacon. It was automated in the 1920s and extinguished in the early 1960s. Shortly thereafter it was demolished. (Lighthouse Digest *archives.*)

The first Grosse Ile North Channel Front Lighthouse was built in 1894 and lasted until 1906 when it was replaced by the structure that is shown here. This lighthouse closely resembles the lighthouse that was once the Strawberry Island Lower Cut Rear Lighthouse in New York. Fortunately, when the lighthouse was no longer needed it did not meet the fate of the wrecking ball, as did its counterparts. In the mid 1960s the local community purchased the lighthouse and the Grosse Isle Historical Society now manages it. Since the lighthouse is surrounded by private property, it is only on rare occasions that the historical society opens the light to the public. (Lighthouse Digest *archives.*)

Mama Juda (Mamajuda) Lighthouses

Wyandotte, Michigan

This may be one of the most unusual names for a lighthouse in America's history. Even to this day, when and how the name was derived is in dispute. A few old records referred to it as Mama Judy. However, depending on what historical records you read, the lighthouse is generally listed as Mama Juda or as one word Mamajuda. Some historians believe the name came from a person who was active in the Underground Railroad who was based in the area to smuggle escaped slaves into Canada. Others believe the name to be a corruption of a French word meaning "grassy shoal." On the other hand, local folklore says the name was in honor of a Native American woman who set up a fishing camp every season at the site many years before the lighthouse was built.

Located in American waters, Mama Juda was a small 30-acre island between Hennepin Point at the north end of Grosse Ile and Fighting Island along the Canadian shore of the Detroit River.

A number of different structures occupied the site over the years as old structures were torn down and rebuilt. The keepers and their families also farmed the land for a source of fresh fruits and vegetables, as did lighthouse keepers at many other family stations around the country.

Maebelle Mason, daughter of Orlo J. Mason, who was the keeper from May, 1885 to June, 1893, was credited with saving the life of a boater. She was awarded life-saving medals from both the U.S. Light House Board and the Shipmasters Association.

By the early 1900s the station was deactivated, and over the years storms have washed away the remains of what was once the home to the lighthouses of Mama Juda.

The first Mama Juda Lighthouse was built in 1849. Its first keeper, David B. Johnson, served here until he resigned in 1853. The lighthouse had one of the magnificent bird-cage style lantern rooms, which, with a few exceptions, has nearly disappeared from the American scene. This structure was torn down in 1866.

35

The second Mama Juda Lighthouse was built in 1866 and was a twin to the Old Mission Point Lighthouse in Traverse City, Michigan. Barney Litogot, who arrived here as the lighthouse keeper in March of 1873, did not serve here for very long; he died in December of that year. He was replaced by his wife Caroline, who continued to serve as the keeper for the next eleven years, even after she had remarried. The last keeper, Thomas Kean, was sent here in January 1911, most likely to deactivate the station, which happened two months after he arrived. The structure no longer stands.

This structure, known as the Mama Juda Range Lighthouse, was built in 1911. It only had two lighthouse keepers in its short existence. Xavier Rains, who arrived in May of 1911, only stayed nine months before being transferred. It is believed that Charles J. Price, who arrived here as the keeper in March of 1912, served here until the lighthouse was discontinued in 1932. The lighthouse was abandoned and eventually lost to the pages of time.

Monroe Lighthouses

Monroe, Michigan

Monroe's first newspaper editor, Edward D. Ellis, was one of those who strongly supported the building of a lighthouse to guide vessels into Monroe Harbor, which was then located in LaPlaisance Bay at the natural mouth of the River Raisin. His letters and editorials worked, because in May of 1828 Congress approved the building of a lighthouse on the west end of Lake Erie at a place known as Otter Creek.

Although there are no known of photographs existing of the first lighthouse, its specifications were the same as a lighthouse that was built in Barcelona, New York that is still standing today. First lit in 1829, its official name was the Otter Creek Lighthouse, but because of its location it was also referred to as the LaPlaisance Bay Lighthouse. It was the first structure to serve as a lighthouse in Monroe, Michigan.

The first keeper was Major John Whipple of Detroit, a veteran of the War of 1812, who served for ten years until he died on duty at the lighthouse.

When a new canal was completed in 1843, it left the Otter Creek Lighthouse four miles away from Monroe Harbor. But it wasn't until 1847 that Congress finally approved the funding for a new lighthouse at a better location. Two years later a new lighthouse was completed and first lighted in September of 1848.

At that time the old Otter Creek Lighthouse was discontinued and sat empty until it was sold in 1854 and dismantled. Parts of the old lighthouse were used to build the foundations of several homes in the area.

The second Monroe Lighthouse was a wooden tower positioned at the mouth of the new canal and rested on the end of the north pier, which stretched one fifth of a mile into Lake Erie. Its official name was the Monroe Pier Lighthouse, but it was also often referred to as the Monroe Harbor Lighthouse.

John Paxton, who became the lighthouse keeper in May of 1853, had an interesting life. During the War of 1812, he was taken prisoner on two separate occasions. The first time, for some reason, he was released, but the second time he escaped and went on to help ferry American forces around Lake Erie. After the war, he married and became the town sheriff from 1827 to 1830. He then opened and owned a grocery store and was also the town's assessor for a few years. He and his wife, Theotiste, had ten children: five boys and five girls. In 1853 he was appointed the lighthouse keeper at the Monroe Pier Lighthouse, a position he held until his death in 1859.

Capt Joseph Guyor, who served as the lighthouse keeper from 1861 to 1865, was also the owner of the Island Hotel, which for many years was the favored resort of hunters and sportsman from all over the country. Known by most at "Uncle Joe," he was reported to be a man of robust constitution who was liked by all.

By the early 1870s, the lighthouse had suffered from wear and age. A report in 1873 stated that "the keeper's house is in a ruinous condition, has no foundation except for a few rotten logs and is now entirely unsafe."

However, the wheels of the government moved slowly and it wasn't until over ten years later that a new lighthouse was built. But the Lighthouse Establishment was frugal and they used much of the lumber from the second lighthouse in building the new third lighthouse to serve Monroe; however it still had the same name: the Monroe Pier Lighthouse. Although major improvements were made at the lighthouse in 1906, it maintained its same basic appearance.

As the area grew, so did its popularity. By the early 1900s, over a hundred boats were participating in the annual July 4th regatta. A two story 225-foot long building called the "Casino" was built by the north pier where famous orchestras played and thousands of people came to dance. A mini amusement park arose, complete with a roller coaster, a merry-go-round and lighted night-time swimming.

Modernization caused the final fate of the third lighthouse at Monroe when, in 1916, a gas light was installed on a skeletal tower on the pier next to the lighthouse and the old station was abandoned. The lighthouse stood until 1922 when it was sold to a man from Toledo. He dismantled it and loaded the lumber on a barge and the remains of the lighthouse were hauled away. No one seems to know what the lumber was used for, or if today there is a building still standing somewhere that was made from the lumber of the third lighthouse in Monroe that once proudly served the mariners of Lake Erie.

The stock market crash of 1929 caused the demise of the tourist attractions by the lighthouse and most of the structures were demolished. Today, hardly a trace remains of the three lighthouses that are now part of the Ghost Lights of Lake Erie.

It is widely believed that the first lighthouse in Monroe, known as the Otter Creek Lighthouse, looked like this structure, which is the Barcelona Lighthouse, formerly known as the Portland Harbor Lighthouse, in Barcelona, New York. (Lighthouse Digest *archives.*)

The second lighthouse to serve Monroe on Lake Erie was a primitive structure by today's standards. Interestingly, the Fresnel lens, although there was room for it, was not centered in the lantern room. When first built, the keeper's house was originally located on shore, but was later moved to the pier. Although the keeper's house was very small and plain, the government tried to improve its appearance with an attractive entryway. The lighthouse station stood until 1885 when it was replaced by a new light station. (Michael Huggins collection, Lighthouse Digest *archives.)*

View from the water of the third and final lighthouse to serve Monroe, Michigan. In this image, the drapes in the lantern room were drawn to protect the Fresnel lens and the brass fittings from the harmful rays of the sun. (Coast Guard photo, Lighthouse Digest *archives.)*

The steamer Newsboy, *built in 1899 by F. W. Wheeler & Company as a freighter, was converted into an excursion boat to transport passengers between Toledo, Ohio and Monroe, Michigan. Displacing 199 gross tons, the wooden hull of the vessel was 104 feet long, 22 feet wide and had a draft of 6 feet 4 inches. It is believed this photograph of the ship docking by the Monroe Lighthouse was taken in 1902. (Michael Huggins collection,* Lighthouse Digest *archives.)*

While rebuilding the piers at Monroe Harbor in 1885, the work crew took a moment to pose for this photograph. The third lighthouse to serve Monroe can be seen in the distance. (Photograph courtesy Monroe County Historical Museum.)

Since the Monroe Lighthouse was on the other pier across from the Casino, the lighthouse keeper could enjoy hearing the music from some of the nation's best orchestras that performed there. The second story of the 225 foot long Casino featured a large open area for ballroom dancing and even roller-skating. In 1927 the building was cut from its moorings and dragged across the ice to the beach to what would become the Sterling State Park in Monroe. (M.N. Gates photo, Michael Huggins collection, Lighthouse Digest *archives*.)

By the 1890s large numbers of people arrived on excursion boats, such as this one, to enjoy the waterfront activities offered in Monroe. Since the vessels docked by the lighthouse, many visitors would often talk and become familiar with the lighthouse keepers who served here over the years. (Monroe County Historical Commission photo, Lighthouse Digest *archives*.)

The regattas hosted by the Monroe Yacht Club drew large crowds for the yearly 4th of July event. The lighthouse can be seen in the distance at the bottom left in the photo. (1907 photograph by M.N. Gates; Michael Huggins collection, Lighthouse Digest *archives*.)

Lighthouse keeper Peter Gussenbauer served at the Monroe lighthouse from 1888 until his death in 1904. Known by nearly everyone as "Uncle Pete," it was written that between Toledo, Ohio and Detroit, Michigan, "there was hardly a sailor or yachtsman that did not know him and, knowing him, esteem him." The *Monroe Democrat* newspaper, in reporting his death, wrote "His inexhaustible fund of humorous stories, his blunt, witty remarks and repartees, his unvarying courtesy to strangers and visitors and cheerful accommodation of all who sought the thousand and one favors that he was in a position to grant, made him scores and scores of friends." He is shown here wearing his official keeper's uniform of the United States Lighthouse Establishment. The letter 'K' on his jacket lapel meant he was the head keeper. (Photograph courtesy Monroe Historical Commission Archives.)

By the time this photograph was taken of the Monroe Lighthouse, its future was doomed. If you look closely you'll notice the Fresnel lens had been removed from the lantern room and replaced by the small beacon atop a skeletal tower sitting on the end of the pier. Notice the round oil storage building. There were a relatively small number of these built and used on the Great Lakes. A few examples of those still standing can be found at Pointe Betsie and South Manitou lighthouses in Michigan. At this time, the abandoned lighthouse was still in relatively

good shape. A man can be seen sitting on the pier fishing with a bamboo pole by the small boat on the pier. Shortly after this photograph was taken, the lighthouse was sold to a private individual who dismantled the historic structure and carted away its lumber. Now lost and nearly forgotten in the dusty pages of time, it is truly one of the Ghost Lights of Lake Erie. (Michael Huggins collection, *Lighthouse Digest* archives.)

Black Rock Lighthouse

Buffalo, New York

Although government records indicated that the Black Rock Lighthouse built in 1856 at the south entrance to the Niagara River near Buffalo, New York, was only built as a temporary structure, it was in use well into 1870. It was replaced by the inhospitable Horseshoe Reef Lighthouse. The rubblestone tower, shown here sat on a pier and contained a 5th order Fresnel lens. It was used in conjunction with another beacon, but photographs of the other aid to navigation seem to be nonexistent.

During its short existence the lighthouse station had only three lighthouse keepers. The last keeper was a woman, Miss Mary E. Lee, who served from October 1869 to September, 1870. It is not known when it was demolished and memories of it have disappeared into the pages of time.

(National Archives photograph.)

Buffalo Lighthouses

Buffalo, New York

The future of the small trading community that started in Buffalo in the late 1700s was marked with the completion of the Erie Canal in 1825. By the early 1900s Buffalo, with its large steel manufacturing base, its railroad hub and grain-milling industry, had grown to the 8th largest city in the United States. All this growth necessitated the construction of a number of lighthouses in Buffalo. Although many of Buffalo's uniquely designed lighthouse structures still stand today, others have been lost.

However, just as the lake-effect snow that Buffalo is famous for disappears, so has much of Buffalo's lighthouse history. And, just as the snow comes back every year, the history of the lighthouses of Buffalo continues to come to the surface.

One of the early structures that served as one of the Buffalo Breakwater Beacons. This structure no longer stands. (Lighthouse Digest *archives.*)

This 1872 Buffalo Breakwater Lighthouse at Buffalo, NY stood on a crib at the end of the breakwater. The structure attached to the lighthouse housed the fog horn machinery, which was also the responsibility of the lighthouse keeper. If you look closely, you will see the fog bell, used as back up, hung from a small pyramid structure on the platform, left of the lighthouse. (Lighthouse Digest *archives.*)

After the 1872 Buffalo Breakwater Light was in use for a time it was decided that the height of its beacon needed to be raised. The entire keeper's quarters were raised to sit upon a new base and the tower itself was raised in height. (Lighthouse Digest *archives.*)

Over the years the old 1872 Buffalo Breakwater Lighthouse had been struck by numerous vessels with each accident necessitating repairs. By the early 1900s it was decided that age, combined with constant repairs, would require the building of a new lighthouse and the old tower was demolished, making it one of the Ghost Lights of Lake Erie. (Lighthouse Digest *archives.*)

By the early 1900s a new Buffalo Breakwater Lighthouse was under construction to replace the 1872 tower that had been demolished.

The structure that was soon to be the Buffalo Breakwater Lighthouse is almost complete. All that is needed to complete the structure are the window shutters, the lantern room and lens. In showing a sense of accomplishment to the work completed thus far, the flag was hoisted at the top of the structure. (Lighthouse Digest *archives.*)

The Buffalo Breakwater Lighthouse in 1914 is completed and ready for service. (Lighthouse Digest archives.)

Veteran lighthouse keepers George Codding and Wilbur Folwell Sr. By the time Codding arrived as a keeper in Buffalo, New York in 1904 he had already seen service at Ashtabula, Vermillion and Oswego lighthouses. Codding stayed in Buffalo until 1913 when he transferred to the Rochester Harbor Beacon Light in Rochester, New York where he served until his retirement in 1940. This photo of the two keepers was taken in Rochester, New York where Folwell also served from 1933 until 1947. (Lighthouse Digest archives.)

The Buffalo Breakwater Lighthouse as it appeared in 1934. James F. Rawson became the keeper here in 1929 and served here until his retirement in 1944. He had three assistant keepers working under his direction. Notice the fog horn protruding from the structure. (U.S. Coast Guard photo, Lighthouse Digest archives.)

Coastguardsman John S. Small at the electric air compressor for the fog signal at the Buffalo Lighthouse in 1954. (Lighthouse Digest archives.)

The lighthouse keepers on duty in July of 1958 received quite a jolt when the Buffalo Breakwater Lighthouse was struck by a freighter. The lighthouse was hit so hard that it moved the crib it was sitting on and caused the entire structure to tilt. It was decided the lighthouse could not be saved. Finally, after sitting in the water tilted for nearly four years, it was demolished in 1961 and became another one of the Ghost Lights of Lake Erie, which has been lost to the dusty pages of time. (U.S. Coast Guard photo, Lighthouse Digest *archives.)*

This unique photograph from 1921 shows the long lost Buffalo Breakwater Lighthouse to the right in the distance. The pyramid style structure in the middle was a Coast Guard lookout tower. The tall tower to the left is the 1833 Buffalo Main Lighthouse, which still stands today. (*U.S. Coast Guard photo,* Lighthouse Digest *archives.*)

Buffalo was also the site of one of the larger of the Lighthouse Depots that were built to service the lighthouses on the Great Lakes. The Buffalo Main Lighthouse, still standing is shown to the right. (Lighthouse Digest *archives.*)

This unique photograph taken in 1955 shows the buildings of the Lighthouse Depot in-between the tall watch tower and the Buffalo Main Light. The watch tower no longer stands. To the far right are shown a large number of Coast Guard vessels. During the era of Prohibition, from 1920 to 1933, the Coast Guard had a large fleet of vessels in Buffalo that were used in an attempt to stop alcohol smuggling from Canada. (U.S. Coast Guard photo, Lighthouse Digest *archives.)*

The interior of lamp shop at the Buffalo Lighthouse Depot where the lenses were assembled, disassembled, and repaired. Interior photos such as this are quite rare. (National Archives photograph.)

Dunkirk Lighthouses

Dunkirk, New York

Dunkirk, New York is home to the beautiful Dunkirk Lighthouse that is managed as the Dunkirk Lighthouse and Veterans Park Museum. People from all over the world come to visit the lighthouse and enjoy the museum and the grounds. But, unless they have paid close attention to the exhibits on display there, they will not know that over the years a number of different lighthouses served on the pier in conjunction with the Dunkirk Lighthouse.

In 1828 a pierhead lighthouse was built to mark the end of the break-water in Dunkirk Harbor. This early 1800s image of the Dunkirk Pierhead Lighthouse shows that the tower was octagon in shape and had one of the old style bird cage lantern rooms. The tower was destroyed by ice floes.

The second Dunkirk Pier Lighthouse as it appeared on June 2, 1911. This tower was built in 1895 to replace the earlier tower that had been destroyed by ice. The structure shown here, no longer stands; it was replaced in 1939 by a pyramidal steel tower. When the steel tower was discontinued it was moved and placed for display on the grounds of the Dunkirk Lighthouse where it can still be viewed today. The site on the pier is now marked by a nondescript smokestack looking aid to navigation. (Lighthouse Digest archives.)

The Dunkirk Lighthouse, which has also been referred to as the Point Gratiot Lighthouse, was commissioned in 1826. At one point the light here was discontinued in favor of the light on the pier, something that was later rectified and both lights were used. In 1876 the tower was totally rebuilt. Francis D. Arnold, who had previously served at the Ashtabula Lighthouse in Ohio and the Presque Isle Beacon Range Lighthouse in Pennsylvania, was assigned here as the 1st assistant keeper in December of 1909. He was promoted to head keeper in April 1928 and served here until his retirement in July 1950 having served a total of 41 years at the Dunkirk Lighthouse. Today the top section of the tower is painted white giving the lighthouse a much different appearance than is shown here. (Lighthouse Digest archives.)

Horseshoe Reef Lighthouse

Buffalo, New York

The Horseshoe Reef Lighthouse, built in 1856, was not built to mark Horseshoe Reef, but instead to warn mariners of the dangers of Middle Reef on Lake Erie on the Canadian and U. S. border. Although the structure had a keeper's living quarters it was only used in inclement weather and the keepers always lived on shore.

The lighthouse was not the most hospitable of stations to be assigned at. Most keepers did not stay long. During its time, 16 keepers resigned, 8 keepers were removed, and most others only stayed long enough to apply or reapply for transfers to another lighthouse. George G. Gilbert, who became the 1st assistant keeper in March of 1871, is the only keeper to have died while assigned to the lighthouse. It was the only lighthouse he had ever worked at.

Another keeper, Jeremiah Crummings, was removed from the job almost as fast as he had been promoted to it. He became the acting 1st assistant keeper on May 24, 1884, a position that was made permanent a few months later in October of that same year. On June 6, 1885 he was promoted to head keeper to replace the acting keeper Henry Higgins who had been removed after only being on the job for less than a month. Crummings did not have the job as head keeper for long. Two months after getting the promotion, he was also removed.

One of the shortest terms of a keeper at the lighthouse was that of Patrick McCabe who

The Horseshoe Reef Lighthouse went into operation in 1856 and it had 4th order Fresnel lens that could be seen for ten miles.

accepted the job of acting assistant keeper on August 28, 1889. He quickly realized this was not the best place to work and quit the following day.

The last person to serve as the keeper, Thomas Joseph, was more tolerable of serving at this location. Thomas arrived here in May, 1902 as the 1st assistant keeper and was promoted to head keeper in April of the following year when Frederick Lawson was transferred and promoted to become head keeper at the Niagara River Range Lighthouse. Thomas stayed on at Horseshoe Reef Lighthouse for nearly 20 years until it was discontinued and replaced in 1920 when a light was placed on top of the Buffalo Water Intake Crib.

By 1930 the Horseshoe Reef Lighthouse had been abandoned by the government and left to elements. Before long, its wood rotted away leaving only a frame structure. It has now deteriorated to the point of beyond being saved. At one point there were discussions to remove the lantern room to have it put on display as an historical artifact. The fact that the iron framework of the structure still stands at the publishing of this book, is in itself somewhat miraculous. For all practical purposes it is a Ghost Light of Lake Erie.

Left to the elements the abandoned the Horseshoe Reef Lighthouse, as shown here, is beyond any hope of ever being saved.

Niagara River Range Lighthouses

Buffalo, New York

Not to be confused with Canadian lighthouses of similar names, the United States built two lighthouses in 1885 on the Upper Niagara River near Buffalo, New York.

The Niagara River Rear Range Lighthouse, established in 1855 was described as a white octagonal tower, pyramid above the first story. It was rebuilt in 1899. The Niagara River Front Range Lighthouse, a 60 foot tall tower was rebuilt in 1900.

Wallace G. Hill arrived here as the station's first lighthouse keeper in June 1885. He joined the United States Lighthouse

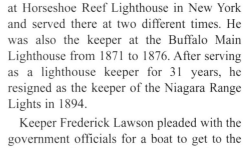

Establishment in October of 1863 as a keeper at Horseshoe Reef Lighthouse in New York and served there at two different times. He was also the keeper at the Buffalo Main Lighthouse from 1871 to 1876. After serving as a lighthouse keeper for 31 years, he resigned as the keeper of the Niagara Range Lights in 1894.

Keeper Frederick Lawson pleaded with the government officials for a boat to get to the lighthouse in inclement wather. After he received the boat he was given permission to spend no more than one dollar a month for a place to store it.

In 1912 the lighthouses were converted to acetylene and put under the care of the keepers of the Buffalo Lighthouse. In 1919 the lighthouses were electrified. In 1925 a lamplighter was hired to keep watch on the lights. However, by 1928 it was recommended that the lights be discontinued when the Peace Bridge, linking Buffalo, New York with Fort Erie, Ontario, was completed.

The Niagara River Front Range Lighthouse, built on the Bird Island Pier, no longer stands and has been lost to the pages of time. (Lighthouse Digest *archives.*)

The Niagara River Rear Range Lighthouse was established in 1885 and was rebuilt in 1899. The lighthouse with its white and black dome lantern room towered over the homes in the area. Later, the lantern room was replaced with a more modern lantern room. When it was discontinued in 1931, it was purchased and moved to Grand Island, New York where it eveunally became the Grand Island Front Range Light. (Lighthouse Digest archives.)

Strawberry Island Range Lighthouses

Strawberry Shoals, New York

In 1908 four range lighthouses of similar design were built on the Upper Niagara River at the Strawberry Shoals about six miles from Buffalo, New York.

Unfortunately, very little has been recorded about the history of the lighthouses and the names of only three people have surfaced who served as keepers of the lighthouses.

In 1912, it was recommended that the lighthouses be downgraded and their keepers were removed. At that time, the care of the Strawberry Island Range Lights and the Niagara River Range Lights were assigned to the keeper of the Buffalo Main Lights.

Today, these lighthouses are truly some of the Ghost Lights of Lake Erie.

The Strawberry Island Upper Cut Rear Range Lighthouse as it appeared in 1921. (U.S. Coast Guard photo, Lighthouse Digest *archives.)*

The Strawberry Island Upper Cut Front Range Lighthouse with the Strawberry Upper Cut Rear Range Lighthouse in the background. (Lighthouse Digest *archives.)*

The Strawberry Island Lower Cut Front Range Lighthouse. (Lighthouse Digest *archives.*)

The Strawberry Island Lower Cut Rear Range Lighthouse. (Lighthouse Digest *archives.*)

The cover of the June 1922 issue of Popular Mechanics Magazine *shows what is believed to be the Strawberry Island Lower Cut Rear Range Lighthouse being barged down the river to a new location which was later discontinued.* (Lighthouse Digest *archives.*)

Ashtabula Lighthouses

Ashtabula, Ohio

Ashtabula has been home to a number of lighthouses over the years. Unfortunately, with the exception of the last one to be built, they no longer stand, having been replaced by nondescript aids to navigation, but without them and the people who served at them, Ashtabula's history would be much different today.

Located about an hour between Cleveland, Ohio and Erie, Pennsylvania, with access to 30 miles of Lake Erie shoreline, Ashtabula became a major shipping and commercial center and, thanks to its lighthouses, has become a city that is rich in maritime and lighthouse history.

Ashtabula's lighthouse history dates back to the early 1800s when the first light, which

was primitive by modern standards, was hung from a broom pole at the harbor's west entrance. The first actual lighthouse to be built dates back to 1836, but the dates of when the other lighthouses were built, moved or torn down can be very confusing to anyone researching these lighthouses. Even the final "real" lighthouse, built on a 50 x 50 foot crib, does not stand at its original location.

The first lighthouse keeper appointed to Ashtabula was Samuel Miniger, who arrived on the scene in May of 1837. Why Miniger left is unclear, but in May of 1838 he was replaced by Jonathan Johnson who quit after only a couple of weeks on the job.

Today Ashtabula's lighthouse history is being kept alive thanks to dedicated volunteers of the Great Lakes Marine and U.S. Coast Guard Memorial Museum (Ashtabula Maritime Museum) that is housed in the former Ashtabula Lighthouse keeper's house, and to the members of the Ashtabula Lighthouse Restoration and Preservation Society that was formed 10 years ago to obtain ownership of the last Ashtabula Lighthouse in order to restore and preserve it for future generations.

The first Ashtabula Lighthouse, built in 1836, was a wooden octagonal structure with what is referred to as a "bird-cage" style lantern room. It no longer stands. (Courtesy Great Lakes Historical Society.)

One of the Ashtabula Pier Lights as it appeared in 1885. The structure was similar to many other lighthouses built on piers and breakwaters on the Great Lakes. The wooden structure no longer stands and has been forgotten in the pages of time. (Lighthouse Digest archives.)

At one time this Ashtabula Lighthouse housed a 4th order Fresnel lens. The lens was removed from the tower and placed in the new Ashtabula Lighthouse that was completed in 1905 and still stands today. This structure no longer stands. (Lighthouse Digest archives.)

This rare image shows the two Ashtabula Pier or Breakwater Lighthouses when they were both still standing. Located directly behind the front lighthouse was the fog signal building which housed all the equipment to operate the fog signal. The vessel shown here was a lighthouse tender, which probably arrived to do some maintenance on the lighthouse or the fog signal equipment. (National Archives photograph.)

With no living quarters in the original Ashtabula lighthouses, the keepers lived on shore in this house, which still stands today as the Great Lakes Marine & U.S. Coast Guard Memorial Museum. The structure is shown here as it appeared in 1904. (U.S. Coast Guard photo, Lighthouse Digest *archives.)*

George V. Codding started his lighthouse career at the Ashtabula Lighthouse in 1896 as the 1st assistant keeper. He served here until March of 1901 when he was transferred and promoted to become the head keeper at the Vermilion Lighthouse in Vermilion, Ohio. In 1904 he was again transferred to become the head keeper at the Buffalo Breakwater South End Lighthouse in Buffalo, NY where he served until he was transferred again in 1913 to become the head keeper at the Rochester Harbor Lighthouse in Rochester, New York. He served in  Rochester until his retirement in 1940. During his lighthouse career, he witnessed in 1910 the transition of our nation's lighthouses from the Light House Board to the Bureau of Lighthouses, more commonly known as the U.S. Lighthouse Service, and finally, in 1939 he saw the Bureau of Lighthouses dissolved and its duties assumed by the United States Coast Guard. (*Lighthouse Digest* archives.)

The Ashtabula West Pierhead Lighthouse in its final days. Having been replaced by a new lighthouse this structure was no longer needed and removed from the site. (Lighthouse Digest *archives.*)

In 1905 the Ashtabula River was widened and a new breakwater was built which resulted in a new lighthouse being built at the end of the breakwater. However, in 1915, the breakwater was extended and the lighthouse, as shown here in 1916, was moved to its new location. After the move was completed, the structure was enlarged. This lighthouse, although no longer at its

original location, still stands today. In 1995 the rotating fourth order Fresnel Lens was removed from the lighthouse for display in the Ashtabula Marine Museum, where in 2006 it was restored by lampist Jim Woodward. Today volunteers of the Ashtabula Lighthouse Restoration and Preservation Society are caring for the lighthouse. (Lighthouse Digest *archives.*)

Frederick J. Hartley, shown here in his United States Lighthouse Establishment uniform, served as the 1st assistant keeper at Ashtabula Lighthouse from January 1904 to March 1907 when he resigned. He served under head keeper Joseph F. Crawford during the transition time when the new lighthouse was built. (Photograph courtesy Ashtabula Lighthouse Restoration and Preservation Society.)

The foundation of the 1905 location of the Ashtabula Lighthouse, which can still be viewed today, is a ghostly reminder of where the lighthouse once stood before being moved in 1916 to the location where it stands today. (Photograph courtesy Ashtabula Lighthouse Restoration and Preservation Society.)

Cedar Point Lighthouses

Sandusky, Ohio

In 1839 a lighthouse was first established on the Cedar Point Peninsula, which is a narrow area that juts out into Lake Erie in Sandusky, Ohio. Named the Cedar Point Lighthouse, it was built under the jurisdiction of Stephen Pleasonton, the 5th Auditor of the Treasury under President Martin Van Bureau. The structure was a rectangular stone dwelling with a lantern room protruding from the top of the house. It was built to mark the eastern approach to Sandusky Bay and Sandusky Harbor.

In 1853 a front range lighthouse was added about 265 feet north of the 1839 structure, at which time the first lighthouse became known as the Cedar Point Rear Range Lighthouse.

By 1867 the original lighthouse had deteriorated with age and was replaced by a similar structure made of brick that also had a lantern room protruding from the center of the house, but it was ten feet higher than the 1839 lighthouse.

Not everyone wanted to be a lighthouse keeper, as was the case with Capt. Astin A Kirby who was offered the job as the Cedar Point Lighthouse keeper on October 7, 1870. Although he took a few days to decide, he turned the job down. Having lived nearly his entire life on ships that operated mostly on Lake Erie, he must have felt that being a lighthouse keeper would have been too con-fining. At the time of his death, at age 86, he was the oldest captain and had served longer than any other ship's captain on the Great Lakes.

Tauman M. Percy, who became the lighthouse keeper in April 1897, had the shortest tenure of any keeper to have served at Cedar Point. He died on the job seven weeks after arriving at the lighthouse.

In 1904 both lighthouses were discontinued, having been replaced by other lighthouses in Sandusky Harbor, and the lantern rooms were reportedly removed.

At that time the front range lighthouse remained standing and was used for the storage of construction material. Local fishermen also stored their nets in the building. On July 4, 1910, the front range lighthouse was destroyed in a spectacular fire. The headline of the following day's newspaper read, "Flames Lick Up Old Lighthouse On Cedar Point." The sub-headline read, "Spectacular Fire is Witnessed By Thousands at Lake Shore Resort." It is widely believed that fireworks set off by passengers on board the excursion steamer *Eastland* were the cause of the fire. However, a former unnamed lighthouse keeper of the light claimed the government deliberately set the fire to get rid of the structure and used the July 4th fireworks as a cover-up.

The last official keeper of the Cedar Point Lighthouse was Daniel Finn. However, responsibilities at that time in 1904 for the maintenance of the old Cedar Point Lighthouse and care of the other minor aids to navigation in the area fell upon Frank Ritter who was the keeper at the nearby Sandusky Bay Lighthouses. During his long career Ritter was credited with saving many lives, but he had plenty of close calls himself. A 'noreaster' once upset Ritter's boat while he was lighting several range light lamps in the harbor. When he and his dog were thrown into the choppy frigid water with its swirling waves and a howling gale force wind, the boat was swept away, leaving nothing for him to cling onto. Fortunately men on the dock heard his screams for help and immediately launched a boat to rescue him. However, his dog was not so lucky. Several days later the animal's body washed up on the shore. At his retirement, in recalling that day, he said it was just one close call among a lot of them during his light keeping years. When Ritter passed away in 1953 he had outlived his wife by 19 years.

In the 1990s, the Cedar Point Amusement Park, known for having more roller coaster rides than any park in the country, purchased the northwest corner of Cedar Point Peninsula for expansion. On this property sat the abandoned building that had once been the Cedar Point Rear Range Lighthouse. Rather than tear the structure down, park management made the momentous decision to restore the historic lighthouse to its original stateliness. Complete with a new lantern room, the restored lighthouse opened to the public in 2001.

The 1838 Cedar Point Lighthouse in Ohio lasted until 1867 when it was demolished to become one of the Ghost Lights of Lake Erie. (Photograph courtesy Great Lakes Historical Society.)

The 1853 Cedar Point Front Range Light sat on pilings jutting out into the water. From this undated photograph, it is unclear where the beacon was displayed. It is also unclear if a keeper lived in the structure. However, it appears it might have been used as a lighthouse supply depot. A fire of mysterious origin destroyed the structure in 1910. (Lighthouse Digest *archives.*)

1789 Lighthouse Service 1939

This 1870s photograph of the Cedar Point Rear Range Light shows the station in its prime. The white picket fence and attractive shutters gave the place a warm homey look. The two unidentified lighthouse keepers in the photograph may have been 1st assistant keeper Joseph A. Gibaut and head keeper Samuel D. Cutcliffe. Daniel Finn came to Cedar Point Lighthouse as the keeper 1901. He had previously been at the Port Clinton Pierhead Lighthouse from February 1900 to October 1900. He was then at the Cleveland East and West Breakwater Lighthouses from October 1900 to October 1901. He resigned as the keeper at Cedar Point in 1904 at the same time the lighthouse was being discontinued. The local newspapers reported at the time that he was moving to Oswego, New York. At that time Frank Ritter, while still maintaining his duties as the keeper of the Sandusky Bay Inner Range Lighthouse, took over as the caretaker of the structure and maintained other aids to navigation in the area. After Cedar Point Lighthouse was discontinued in 1904 its lantern room was removed shortly thereafter. (*Lighthouse Digest* archives.)

The dilapidated former Cedar Point Rear Range Lighthouse as it appeared in August of 2000. Shortly thereafter it was restored by the Cedar Point Amusement Park. (Photograph by Wayne Sapulski, Maritime Photographic Co.)

The restored Cedar Point Lighthouse is on the grounds of the Cedar Point Amusement Park. The tower and lantern room are a reproduction. (Julie A. Lake, Lighthouse Digest archives.)

Cleveland Lighthouses

Cleveland, Ohio

Cleveland is named after General Moses Cleaveland who first charted the region in 1792. It didn't take long for this area to grow and eventually become an important port on the shores of Lake Erie. At some point, the spelling of the name was simplified from Cleaveland to Cleveland.

Anyone attempting to tell the story of the lighthouses of Cleveland, Ohio would have to write an entire book. Although there are lighthouses still standing in Cleveland, most people are unaware of the numerous previous lighthouses and other aids to navigation that once graced the city's waterfront, which are now among the Ghost Lights of Lake Erie, having been lost to the pages of time.

Cleveland's lighthouse history dates back to 1830 when the first beacon was constructed. Although no longer standing, it was the beginning of the amazing history of the Lighthouses of Cleveland. Many of

Cleveland's lighthouses were built on the numerous breakwaters and piers that were constructed and reconstructed in the harbor. In many cases, the old records of the lighthouses can be difficult to interpret and are even sometimes contradictory. However this does not distract from the historical importance of these lighthouses and the men and women who tended them, in many cases, with great sacrifice in the protection of human life.

This early image of Cleveland's first lighthouse, named the Cleveland Main Light, built in 1871-72, is believed to have been taken in 1859. It replaced an earlier lighthouse at this site. It has long been lost to the pages of time. (Lighthouse Digest *archives.*)

The first Cleveland East Pier Lighthouse was an open frame tower with exposed stairs to the lantern room. The lighthouse worked in conjunction with the Cleveland Main Light. However, this structure, with its exposed stairway, made tending the beacon very difficult in inclement weather. Built in 1832, it lasted until 1851 when it was removed and replaced by another structure. (Lighthouse Digest *archives.*)

This 40-foot hexagonal structure replaced the open frame East Pier Lighthouse in 1851. It no longer stands. (National Archives photograph.)

In 1872, the government built this elaborate Victorian Gothic style structure to replace the original Cleveland Main Lighthouse. It was built on the same property as the original lighthouse. The home was a duplex to accommodate living quarters for the lighthouse keeper and the assistant keeper and their families. The tower was an amazing 84-foot high. At that time there were many other impressive homes in the neighborhood. When the tower was removed 1895, parts of it were used to build the Braddock Point Lighthouse in New York, which was of similar design. (Lighthouse Digest *archives.*)

After the tower was removed from Cleveland Main Lighthouse, the keeper's house remained standing and, for the next 32 years, continued to be used as housing for the lighthouse keepers in Cleveland. By the time this photograph was taken in 1910, the once beautiful homes in the neighborhood were long gone and had been replaced by commercial buildings and warehouses. The old former keeper's house was torn down in 1936 to make way for the Main Avenue Bridge. (Courtesy Great Lakes Historical Society.)

This early image of the Cleveland Beacon Lighthouse which stood at the end of the west pier shows a lighthouse keeper to the left and a man in the middle who is most likely a lighthouse inspector. In the distance to the right is the Cleveland West Breakwater Lighthouse. Neither of the structures are standing today. Barely visible, in the middle is the still standing Cleveland Harbor West Pierhead Lighthouse, now known as the Cleveland Main Entrance Light. (National Archives photograph.)

This structure, referred to as one of the Cleveland Beacons, once stood on the east pier. It was typical of many of the lighthouses of the time that were built on piers and breakwaters. (National Archives photograph.)

Early image of the Cleveland East Pierhead Lighthouse. The lighthouse rested atop four concrete squares. It is no longer standing. (Lighthouse Digest archives.)

This structure, identified on the photo only as a Cleveland Beacon, almost looks homemade. It is believed to be one of the structures that served on west end of the East Breakwater. (National Archives photograph.)

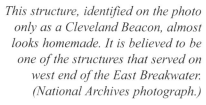

The Cleveland Breakwater West End Lighthouses. Since neither of these structures have a light, they may have been discontinued by the time this photograph was taken. In the distance can be seen the Cleveland West Breakwater Lighthouse. Since a sailing vessel of some kind can be seen sunk in the water, this photo may have been taken after a storm. (U.S. Coast Guard photo, Lighthouse Digest *archives.)*

This early 1900s image shows the skeleton tower on the west pier and the wooden tower on the east pier in the distance. (U.S. Coast Guard photo, Lighthouse Digest *archives.)*

The lighthouse tower shown here originally stood in Rochester, New York. It was recycled and moved to Cleveland, where in 1885, after modifications, it became the Cleveland West Breakwater Lighthouse. Since the breakwater was not connected to the shore, the keepers had to row to the lighthouse. The station's boat house was of an unusual design, allowing the boat to be raised and stored into the side of the structure. (Lighthouse Digest *archives.*)

This view of the Cleveland West Breakwater Lighthouse clearly shows the large fog whistle system at the lighthouse and the fog bell that was used as backup should the fog whistle (horn) system fail. Showing that some thought went onto the construction, the false doors on the boat house look real but did not open. The boat was raised into the boathouse from the side of the structure as previously shown. (Lighthouse Digest *archives.*)

Because of complaints about the visibility of the Cleveland West Breakwater Lighthouse, in 1903 the government raised the entire tower up and placed it upon a new base made of timber. The work crew must have had nerves of steel when they posed for this photo. One false move for any of them would have resulted in serious injury if not death. Later reports told of how the weight of the entire structure, with its poor foundation under the crib, would often sway, giving concern to the keepers that the entire structure might simply lean and collapse into the water. It was eventually decided that the lighthouse needed to be replaced. (U.S. Coast Guard photo, Lighthouse Digest *archives.)*

The Cleveland East Pier Lighthouse as it appeared in the late 1800s. The walkway on the pier allowed for safe access to and from the lighthouse in inclement weather, especially when waves would crash over the pier. (Lighthouse Digest *archives.*)

The Cleveland West Pier Lighthouse was a round conical tower that stood at the end of the pier near the Cleveland United States Life-Saving Service Station. The Life Saving Service, along with the Revenue Cutter Service, was merged in 1915 to create the United States Coast Guard. In 1939 the U.S. Lighthouse Service was dissolved and its duties were taken over by the Coast Guard. This lighthouse no longer stands; however a replica of it was built in 1997 near Nautica Entertainment. (U.S. Coast Guard photo, Lighthouse Digest *archives.)*

Early view of the Cleveland West Pier Lighthouse. In the distance can be seen the Cleveland West Breakwater Lighthouse. (Lighthouse Digest *archives.*)

Frederick T. Hatch, shown here in his U.S. Lighthouse Service uniform, formerly served as a Surfman for the U.S. Life Saving Service at the Cleveland station. He received appointment as the Head Lighthouse Keeper at the Cleveland Breakwater Light in 1884, which in 1910 had its name changed to the Cleveland West Pierhead Lighthouse. Hatch has the distinction of having received two Gold Life Saving Medals for two separate acts of heroism. (Lighthouse Digest *archives.*)

This is one of the early Cleveland Water Intake Crib Lighthouses from an image taken in 1870 shortly before the lighthouse was officially lit as an aid to navigation. It was built on the second intake to serve the city. Records indicate the keeper, who was provided living quarters at the site, was assigned here for nine months a year. The year when the tower was demolished is unclear. (Photograph courtesy Western Reserve Historical Society and Archives.)

A full-fledged lighthouse tower was placed atop this Cleveland Water Intake Crib, which was completed in 1904. Although there is still a beacon and fog horn at the site, this tower was removed years ago. (National Archives photograph.)

Conneaut Harbour Lighthouses

Conneaut, Ohio

Because many old records have conflicting information or in some cases disappeared altogether, many historians can't agree on just exactly how many lighthouses have stood in Conneaut, which is the northeastern most part of Ohio. However, as is evident by old photographs there were a number of lighthouses of various designs that were built over the years to mark the entrance into the harbor. As is the case with many lighthouses, as time goes on, more of the history of these lighthouses will be discovered. The first lighthouses were established here in 1835 during the presidency of Andrew Jackson.

The year that this early image was taken of one of the Conneaut Lighthouse with a large sailing vessel is unknown. But on the back of the photo was written the following two words, "built 1935." (Photograph courtesy Carolyn Barrett collection, Lighthouse Digest *archives.)*

A close up of one of the early Conneaut Breakwater Lights shows that it was only a open wooden structure with a lantern on top of it. Barely visible in the background to the left is another early lighthouse. (Lighthouse Digest *archives*)

This old and blurred image barely shows one of very early Conneaut Harbor Breakwater Lights. (Lighthouse Digest *archives.*)

This 1885 photograph is the shorter of the Conneaut Pier Lighthouses. The walkway had been built to assist the keeper in access to and from the tower in times of inclement weather when it was not uncommon for waves to wash over the breakwater. (Lighthouse Digest archives.)

Image of the taller of the two early breakwater lighthouses at Conneaut, Ohio. The area is bustling with industrial activity and a number of people can be seen fishing and relaxing by the lighthouse. (Lighthouse Digest archives.)

Since there were no living quarters at the early Conneaut Breakwater Lighthouses, this home was constructed on the mainland for the keepers and their families to live in. (Lighthouse Digest *archives.*)

Thick black smoke billows from the freighters and the tug boats at the entrance to Conneaut Harbor. One of the lighthouses is to the left. Vintage post cards such as this are often times among the best recorded images of an area. (Lighthouse Digest *archives.*)

Lighthouse at Conneaut Harbor, Ohio.

In the 1890s the government built this solid lighthouse at the end of one of the Conneaut Piers. One of the keepers took a moment out of his schedule to pose for the photographer. Sadly this structure no longer stands. (Lighthouse Digest archives.)

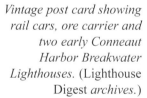

Vintage post card showing rail cars, ore carrier and two early Conneaut Harbor Breakwater Lighthouses. (Lighthouse Digest archives.)

In the early 1900s the Lighthouse Service constructed this elaborate lighthouse at Conneaut, Ohio. This 1920 photograph indicates there was plenty of room to house the mechanical equipment required to maintain the station as well as living quarters. In 1936 the lighthouse was blown up and replaced by a modern deco art style lighthouse. If this structure were still standing today it could have been a combination museum and bed and breakfast. *Although photographs must have been taken of its demise, they continue to remain elusive.* (Lighthouse Digest *archives.*)

Although this lighthouse still stands at Conneaut, Ohio today, the historic lantern room along with its beautiful Fresnel lens, as shown in this 1948 photograph, has been removed and replaced by a modern beacon atop the tower. Edward Pfister, the lighthouse keeper for many years recalled in 1935 when the tower was completed that it was much different from the wooden tower that was here when he started his job in Conneaut in 1894. (Lighthouse Digest archives.)

Vintage post cards are often the only images available of some light-houses and are often beneficial to lighthouse historians and historical researchers. However, in this case, this post card published by Bruce Gardner of Geneva, Ohio, the company used some artistic license and showed two twin art deco style towers. However, there never were twin towers of this style in Conneaut, Ohio.

The tombstone of Conneaut Lighthouse keeper Ephrain Capron at the City Cemetery in Conneaut, Ohio. Capron served as the lighthouse keeper from July 1849 to April 16, 1843 when he resigned for unknown reasons. He was replaced by Whitney Grant who served until May 1861. At that time Capron was reappointed as the lighthouse keeper under the administration of President Abraham Lincoln and he held the job until May 1869 when he was removed, probably for political reasons. In describing his life in his obituary of October 29, 1884, the *Conneaut Reporter* newspaper wrote, "He endured all the hardships incident to the pioneer life in this country. In his younger days he followed the lakes in the various capacities of sailor, mate, and master and in the prime of his life he was regarded as one of the reliable and trusty captains for which our town has ever been known for." The newspaper went on to tell how Mr. Capron was a good citizen, a Christian gentleman, a kind husband, and an indulgent father. (Photograph by Carolyn Barrett.)

The Dean of Lake Erie

The local newspapers labeled Edward Pfister, "The Dean of the Lake Erie Light Keepers." Pfister joined the United States Lighthouse Service in 1892 as an assistant keeper at the Presque Isle Beacon Range Lighthouse in Erie Pennsylvania. He was transferred and promoted as head keeper at Conneaut in 1894 to replace lighthouse keeper John Starkey who had been the keeper since 1885 and had died of skin cancer.

Pfister remained as the head keeper of the Conneaut Lighthouses for the next 43 years. Most of the time, Pfister had two assistant keepers working under him. He retired on March 31, 1937 just a few weeks after signing his retirement papers in his hospital bed where he had been recovering from kidney problems and a hip injury. Although he was supposed to have retired two years earlier, he had decided to stay on, especially since the government did not insist that he retire. He said, in referring to the new lighthouse and automation, "Why quit, they finally made everything so easy that there isn't any work to do anymore." At that time he recalled the many previous years where he had witnessed every possible change imaginable at any lighthouse on the Great Lakes. Towers came and went, equipment came and went, and he was on duty when the first fog horn was installed. During all this time and while constantly trying to learn about all the new equipment being installed, and overseeing the demolition of old towers and the construction of new towers, he risked his life on many occasions to get to and from the lighthouses in inclement weather to keep the lights shining.

In 1922 Pfister was honored by the government for saving the lives of six crewmen of the *Lighter Newman*. In a winter gale with strong winds and high waves, and with no power boat available, Pfister rowed the lighthouse skiff out to rescue the men from the foundering vessel. Once back at the lighthouse he dragged the half frozen men over the ice covered break-wall into the lighthouse. The men were stranded inside the lighthouse for two days until the storm abated. (*Lighthouse Digest* archives.)

Fairport Harbor Lighthouses

Fairport, Ohio

A great destination for the true light-house buffs is Fairport Harbor, Ohio; the area is packed with lighthouse history. Located midway between Cleveland and Ashtabula on Lake Erie, Fairport Harbor is a large manmade harbor that protects the mouth of the Grand River. The village of Grand River, with a population of around 450 people, lies on the west bank and the village of Fairport Harbor, with a population of around 2800 people, lies on the east bank of the river. It is here in Fairport Harbor where one can visit one of the first and oldest museums in the United States to be housed in lighthouse.

The first lighthouse established here was in 1825 and its first lighthouse keeper was Henry Phelps. However, he did not stay long and resigned after serving a little over 10 months.

This structure, known as the Grand River Beacon, on the East Pier at the mouth of the Grand River at Fairport Harbor, Ohio, was built in the 1830s. At that time there was no breakwater. This lighthouse and the lighthouse on the hill were used as a range for ships entering the harbor from the west. Although this tower was primitive by more modern standards, it had one of the old style beautiful "bird-cage" style lantern rooms. The lighthouse keeper standing by the lighthouse may have either James McAdams or George Rogers. The structure, which was long ago lost to the pages of time, is truly one of the Ghost Lights of Lake Erie. (Lighthouse Digest archives.)

The second keeper was Samuel Butler, an enterprising businessman and politician, who was also an active abolitionist. For some reason, perhaps political, he resigned as the keeper in February 1833. He returned again as the keeper in August of 1839 and remained until May of 1845 when he resigned again. He owned the Eagle Tavern, which was often used as a meeting place for other abolitionists and as a safe house and terminal of the "Underground Railway" before the War Between the States. Butler summoned the services of anti-slavery ship captains to transport the slaves across Lake Erie to Canada. When he couldn't find a captain available, he would then take charge of a vessel and pilot the boat himself. When he died in 1881 at the age of 87, the local newspaper described him as the last of the old pioneers who had helped in the growth of the area.

In 1868 it was reported that the lighthouse was in such bad shape that it had to be discontinued, and a light was established on a temporary tower. A new lighthouse was finally completed and first lit on August 11, 1871.

Captain Joseph Babcock was the first keeper at the new station. He himself led such an interesting life prior to becoming keeper that a movie could have been made about him. At the age of 8, he had escaped death in an Indian attack because his mother was Indian. Before becoming the lighthouse keeper, he served an illustrious career in the Civil War. Two of his children were born at the lighthouse and one of them, a son, died of smallpox at the lighthouse. Another son, Daniel, grew up to become the assistant keeper from 1901 to 1919, and then head keeper until the lighthouse was decommissioned in 1925.

It was reported that Captain Joseph Babcock's wife spent a long period of time ill and bedridden on the second floor at the lighthouse. She kept a number of cats to comfort her and help her pass the time.

For a number of years, Paula Brent, a curator who lived at the museum, had reported seeing the ghost of a gray cat. She told local newspaper reporter Magi Martin in an interview, "It would skitter across the floor near the kitchen, like it was playing. I would catch glimpses of it from time to time. Then one evening I felt its presence when it jumped on the bed. I felt its weight pressing on me. At first it kind of freaked me out. But ghosts don't bother me. They are part of the world."

Obviously many people thought she was imagining things or perhaps dreaming. However, in a story worthy of "Ripley's Believe It or Not," those people must have quickly changed their minds when they heard that a work crew, installing air conditioning vents for the museum at the old lighthouse, found the mummified remains of a cat in a crawl space beneath the lighthouse.

In 1925, the lighthouse was discontinued and darkened in favor of a new lighthouse and fog signal station, which was installed on the west breakwater pierhead and established on June 9, 1925.

The new breakwater lighthouse was fabricated in Buffalo, New York and transported by barge to Fairport Harbor. However, the actual tower and lantern room were actually built on the station when it arrived in Fairport Harbor.

Over the years there were a number of other breakwater structures that were also taken care of by the keeper of the Fairport Harbor Lighthouse.

In the meantime, orders came from Washington to tear down the old Fairport Harbor Lighthouse. However, local protests were loud and clear, so the government backed down and left the building standing. But it remained standing as an abandoned relic of another time. When the Coast Guard took over the Lighthouse Service in 1939, they also talked of tearing it down; there was simply no reason for them to keep it. Again, local protests were loud and clear, but this time there was a plan for the structure — a museum.

Today, the Fairport Historical Society runs the Fairport Harbor Marine Museum at the lighthouse.

Attached to the old lighthouse and museum is the pilothouse of the Great Lakes freighter *Frontenac*. This in itself is the kind of tale that makes lighthouse history so fascinating to study. The *Frontenac* is the same ship that, in July of 1958, smashed into New York's Buffalo Breakwater Lighthouse, knocking it 20 feet backwards and caused it to have a 15 to 20 degree tilt. Amazingly, the Buffalo Breakwater Lighthouse, later torn down, was a near twin to the current Fairport Harbor West Breakwater Pierhead Lighthouse.

The original Fairport Harbor Lighthouse was known as the Grand River Lighthouse. Built in 1825, it remained in use until 1869. It is now one of the Ghost Lights of Lake Erie. (Great Lakes Historical Society.)

The Notice to Mariners, dated March 29, 1875, described the beacon at Fairport Harbor East Pier as being "a frame structure, square in plan, painted black below and white above." It was illuminated by a 6th order lens and displays a fixed white light. It no longer stands. (Lighthouse Digest *archives.*)

This iron lighthouse tower was located on the West Pier at Fairport Harbor. Look closely and you will see the West Breakwater in the background. It appears that the men were making some type of repairs to the structure. (Lighthouse Digest *archives.*)

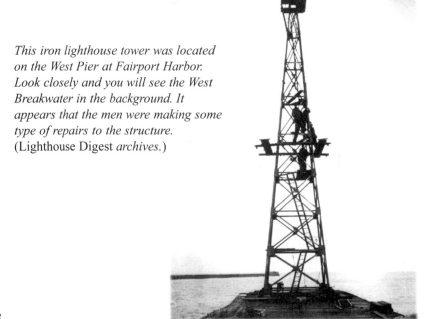

Fairport Harbor West Breakwater Lighthouse prior to 1925. Notice the lighthouse keeper and the ice buildup on the breakwater. (National Archives photograph.)

The Fairport Harbor Lighthouse, also known as the Grand River Lighthouse, as it appeared in 1910. Built in 1871 to replace the original 1825 lighthouse, it remained in use until 1925 when the Fairport Harbor West Breakwater Lighthouse replaced it. The structure, still standing today, houses the Fairport Harbor Marine Museum. (Lighthouse Digest archives.)

Captain Joseph Babcock served as keeper at the Fairport Harbor Lighthouse in 1871 and served here until his retirement in 1919. When Babcock started at the lighthouse, Civil War General Ulysses S. Grant was President and by the time he retired, World War I, which changed the world forever, was over and Woodrow Wilson was President. His son, Daniel, who had been assistant keeper since April of 1901, succeeded him as head keeper. (Photograph courtesy Fairport Historical Society.)

Daniel Babcock, following in his father's foot-steps, joined the United States Lighthouse Service and in 1901 he became the assistant lighthouse keeper of the Fairport Harbor Lighthouse. He served in that position until 1919 when he succeeded his father as head lighthouse keeper upon his father's retirement. In 1925, when the Fairport Harbor Lighthouse was discontinued, he became the first keeper of the new Fairport Harbor West Pierhead Lighthouse. Apparently life at the new light-house did not suit him and he retired after only being at the new station for three months. He is shown here in the white summer dress uniform, that although was not widely used, was an approved uniform of the lighthouse keepers United States Lighthouse Service. (Photograph courtesy Fairport Historical Society.)

The 65-ton base of the Fairport Harbor West Breakwater Lighthouse was transported from Buffalo, New York for the 147-mile long trip to Fairport Harbor, Ohio in June of 1921. The structure was prefabricated at the Buffalo Lighthouse Depot in Buffalo, New York. The lantern room would be added later. The lighthouse and fog signal structure was completed in 1925. (Photograph courtesy Fairport Historical Society.)

The Fairport Harbor West Breakwater Lighthouse is shown here in 1922 when it was still under construction. A temporary light was used until a beacon could be installed in the lantern room. This light-house still stands today and is privately owned. (Lighthouse Digest *archives.*)

Green Island Lighthouses

Put-in-Bay, Ohio

Green Island Lighthouse was established in 1855 at the west end of Green Island, a small 15-acre island one mile west of Bass Island in the western part of Lake Erie.

The island itself gained prominence in the early 1800s when crystallized celestite, or Strontian, was discovered in the cliffs on the island. It became the principle American source of specimens of celestite for mineralogical collection throughout the world. In geological literature, it became known as "Strontian Island." However, by 1898 the supply of crystals was exhausted and the islands second named disappeared into the pages of time.

The first lighthouse built on the island didn't last long, but not because it wasn't well built. A fast moving fire on a blistery cold New Year's Eve on December 31, 1863 destroyed the lighthouse. When the fire first started, lighthouse keeper, Col. Charles F. Drake, and his wife Mary, tried to fight the fire, but soon realized the battle was fruitless. The keeper, realizing that the storm, with its gale force winds, would likely delay any help in reaching the island, was badly burned while trying to save items that would help keep the family warm.

From the mainland, the locals, knowing there was no immediate way to reach the island during the storm, watched in horror as they saw the flames and smoke billowing from the island. Among those watching was the son of the lighthouse keeper who led the rescue effort the following day. When rescuers were finally able to reach the island they found the keeper, with his wife and daughter, cramped inside the station's outhouse where they had put a featherbed over their bodies in an attempt to keep from freezing to death. When the family was rescued, they were suffering from hypothermia, frost bite and burns, but eventually they all made a full recovery. A new lighthouse was built and completed in July 1865.

Civil War veteran Joseph A. Gibaut became the Green Island Lighthouse keeper in October of 1882. He had previously been stationed at the Sandusky Bay Inner Lighthouse from 1879 to 1882. During his tenure as the lighthouse keeper at Green Island Lighthouse his assistant was a relative, Mrs. L. Gibaut, who died while on duty in November 1898. Joseph Gibaut stayed on at Green Island until April of the following year when he resigned. When Gibaut died in 1933 the newspapers described him as one of the early pioneers of traveling by automobile for sightseeing. He was also one of the first people to own and operate an automobile rental business.

George Fergueson, who arrived at the lighthouse as its keeper in June 1905, remained for six years. He was transferred in

February 1914 to Fort Niagara Lighthouse on Lake Ontario, New York where he remained until 1928. A local newspaper, in describing his time on Green Island, reported that "his faithful wife had been his only companion on the isolated island."

Another keeper had "a splendid team of greyhound dogs who made daily trips in the wintertime pulling a sled across the ice with the keeper's children, transporting them to and from school on the mainland." In today's modern age of rules and regulations, it is highly doubtful that, if there were still lighthouse keepers, the government would allow such a practice.

A small barn was erected on the island for the keeper's livestock, which included a three acre fenced-in pasture. Chickens were also raised by the keeper, which offered a fresh supply of eggs and meat for the family.

However, time caught up with the Green Island Lighthouse and in 1926 the Bureau of Lighthouses (United States Lighthouse Service) removed the keepers and automated the lighthouse. However the light itself continued to remain in the tower until 1939 when the Coast Guard took over the Lighthouse Service. They removed the light in the tower and replaced it with a small beacon atop a steel open frame erector-style tower nearby. The old lighthouse was then abandoned and left to the elements.

Eventually the island was turned over to the U.S. Fish & Wildlife Service and is now managed by the Ohio Department Natural Resources as a wildlife refuge that is off limits to the general public.

Unfortunately the second Green Island Lighthouse met the same fate as the first Green Island Lighthouse, only this time it was vandals who started the fire that literally gutted the old structure. Today what is left of the lighthouse station is overgrown with brush and trees. Like many of the Mayan and Inca ruins of Central and South America, the vegetation has obliterated the lighthouse remains to the extent that most people will never know this was once one of Lake Erie's historic lighthouse stations.

This is a rare old image of the first Green Island Lighthouse of Lake Erie, Ohio, which was destroyed by a fire on December 31, 1863. (Lighthouse Digest archives.)

The second Green Island Lighthouse completed in July, 1865 is shown here in its prime. This image shows a barn for the keeper's livestock and clearly shows that the drapes were drawn in the tower to protect the valuable Fresnel lens from the harmful rays of the sun. Notice that the trees are not very large. Today the area is nearly obscured by over-growth. (Lighthouse Digest *archives.*)

Although the date of this photo-graph is unknown, by the time this image was taken of the Green Island Lighthouse, vines had grown on the side of the keeper's house and the tower. Also, a summer porch had been added to the back of the struc-ture. (Photograph courtesy Great Lakes Historical Society.)

This image of the Green Island Light Station boat clearly shows the letters USLHE, which stands for United States Lighthouse Establishment before the name changed to United States Lighthouse Service. The canopy for the boat was likely made by lighthouse keeper George Fergueson who mailed this image to his friend, Captain D. D. Hill, at the Crossover Lighthouse Station in New York. (Judi Kearney collection, Lighthouse Digest *archives.)*

When this aerial image of Green Island Lighthouse was taken, the light had been removed from the tower and placed on the steel skeleton tower shown to the right. Since then, this steel tower has been replaced by a different tower. When vandals set the lighthouse on fire, the interior of the lighthouse was gutted and the roof collapsed. (U.S. Coast Guard photo, Lighthouse Digest *archives.)*

Huron Harbor Lighthouse

Huron, Ohio

Huron was first settled in 1792 when a trading post was established on the west bank of the Huron River. Growth was rapid and by the 1830s, the town was a major ship building center on Lake Erie which necessitated the building of a lighthouse in 1835. This early tower lasted until 1854 when a fierce spring storm toppled the structure. It wasn't until three years later that a new tower was built at the end of the pier, which extended into the harbor. This lighthouse was an open-frame structure with a totally exposed spiral staircase that led to the lantern room. This proved to be a mistake and it was difficult and sometimes impossible and dangerous to service the light in inclement weather. There was no living quarters at the lighthouse, requiring the lighthouse keeper to live on shore in government provided housing. By 1865 the government enclosed the base of the tower to make it safer for the keeper to tend the lighthouse.

This rare view of the second Huron Harbor Lighthouse with the lighthouse keeper standing outside the lantern room. This image was taken long before the lower base of the tower was enclosed and an entryway door was added in 1914. The keeper's house no longer stands.

By the 1930s a new breakwater had been built and it was decided to build another lighthouse at the end of the new breakwater and it became known as the Huron Harbor East Breakwater Lighthouse and the old tower was called the Huron Harbor West Pier Lighthouse. The newer lighthouse, completed in 1936 reflected the so-called "Art Deco" style of the time and was a near twin to the lighthouse built in Conneaut, Ohio.

Exactly when it was decided that the old west pier light was no longer needed is unclear, but it was eventually torn down leaving only the modern structure. In 1972, for reasons still unclear to most, the Coast Guard removed the lantern room from the Art Deco tower and installed a modern solar powered beacon atop the tower.

An early image of the second Huron Harbor Lighthouse taken shortly after the lighthouse was built.

It must have been off-season when this photo of the Huron Harbor West Pier was taken. In the summer months the pier was often busy with sightseers or people fishing. The large structure to the left is a round steel oil storage shed was a style that was apparently only used at selected lighthouses on the Great Lakes.

The Huron Harbor West Pier Lighthouse, shown here no longer stands.

*The base of the Huron Harbor Lighthouse
that the new 1935 "Art-Deco" lighthouse
tower would stand upon, as was its twin in
Conneaut, Ohio, were built in Buffalo, New
York and then floated by barge to their new
homes. This square base was then lifted up
and put on a cement crib and the tower was
then built on top of the base.*

*This "Art-Deco" style lighthouse was built in Huron Harbor in 1935. Similar
style structures were built in Conneaut, Ohio, Port Washington, Wisconsin,
Indiana Harbor, Indiana and for the Keweenaw Upper Entrance Lighthouse
in Michigan. Although this lighthouse still stands today, its historic lantern
room was removed, which altered the historical integrity of the tower.*

Lorain Lighthouses

Lorain, Ohio

Off shore of Lorain in Lake Erie, stands the rugged and picturesque Lorain West Breakwater Lighthouse that has become the symbol of Lorain. However, few will ever know about the other lighthouses that once stood near here.

The first settlement here, at the mouth of the Black River, which dates back to 1807 was known as Mouth of the Black River, which was later shortened to Black River. When the area was incorporated in 1834 its name was changed to Charleston. When the area was re-incorporated 40 years later the name was changed to Lorain.

The first beacon here, as was typical in many parts of the country, was nothing more than a lantern hanging from, a pole near the mouth of the Black River. As shipping increased it became obvious that the area needed a real lighthouse and the first structure was built close to shore in the late 1830s.

In 1875 when a new 600 foot pier was constructed on the west side of the mouth of the Black River a new lighthouse was placed at the end of the pier.

Over time the pier was often damaged by ship collisions and various changes were made to the range lighthouses that stood on the pier.

This structure was known as the Black River Lighthouse in Lorain, Ohio. The brick and stone lighthouse no longer stands and is now one of the Ghost Lights of Lake Erie. (Lighthouse Digest archives.)

111

The Lorain West Pierhead Lighthouse was a wooden structure that stood elevated off the pier. Before an elevated walkway was built several keepers were washed off the pier while attempting to service the lighthouse. Reportedly, at least one keeper lost his life in the line of duty at the lighthouse. The structure is long gone, having been lost in the pages of time. (Photograph courtesy Black River Historical Society.)

This duplex served as the on-shore home for the lighthouse keepers and their families. The home was quite nice by government standards and appeared to be a comfortable place to live. Each keeper's family had private entrances on each side of the structure. (Lighthouse Digest archives.)

The Lorain West Breakwater Lighthouse as it appeared in 1919 shortly after it was constructed and before the breakwater was built. The three story lighthouse was built on a wooden crib foundation. Living quarters for the keepers was on the second floor. In the 1960s the lighthouse was decommissioned and the Coast Guard planned to tear the structure down. Local last minute initiatives and a stroke of luck saved the lighthouse. Now restored, this beautiful monument to the past has been saved for future generations. (Lighthouse Digest *archives.*)

Manhattan Range Lighthouses

Toledo, Ohio

So little information exists on the Manhattan Range Lighthouses, it's almost as if they never existed at all.

In 1895 the government built two range lighthouses to mark the middle line of a new straight channel into Toledo Harbor Ohio.

At some point the original wooden lighthouses featured here were demolished. They were replaced by two nearly identical looking structures with square metal lantern rooms that rested atop four iron legs. They were also both later discontinued. Although they still exist today, they are both now privately owned, having been moved to new locations where they no longer serve as lighthouses.

The original Manhattan Rear Range Lighthouse was a beautifully built structure. The first lighthouse keeper was Harvey H. Dayan who served here from March 1895 to July 1905, when, for reasons not clear, he resigned his position. He was followed by Edward Ahart, who had previously been the 1st assistant keeper at the Buffalo Breakwater North End Lighthouse in New York for ten years. Ahart served here for the next 21 years until his retirement in June of 1926. No longer standing, it is one of the Ghost Lights of Lake Erie.

It appears the two gentlemen in this photo had on their Sunday best when they posed for this photo in front of the Manhattan Rear Range Lighthouse. With it attractive lighthouse this could have been turned into a first class bed and breakfast. Everything about the station was in immaculate order when this image was taken. (National Archives photograph.)

The original Manhattan Front Range Lighthouse was a short tower that rested on a man-made foundation in the water, connected to the mainland by a walkway. This structure no longer stands, having been lost in the pages of time. It is now one of the Ghost Lights of Lake Erie.

Marblehead Lighthouse

Marblehead, Ohio

Today Marblehead Lighthouse is one of the most popular lighthouses on Lake Erie as well as on the Great Lakes. It is home to a wonderful museum, is visited and photographed by thousands of tourists from all over the world and it is even featured on an Ohio automobile license plate. Although it is not the oldest lighthouse structure on the Great Lakes, it is however the oldest lighthouse to be in continuous operation.

Because the lighthouse looks significantly different today from when it was built in 1821, its original tower is worthy of being considered as one of the Ghost Lights of Lake Erie. Its first keeper was Benjamin Wolcott whose home still stands to this day near the lighthouse. Upon his death, his wife Rachel took over his job as the keeper of the light. Interestingly, the third keeper of the lighthouse, Loderick Brown married Margaret Kelly, whose father, William Kelly, was the contractor who built the lighthouse.

When the lighthouse was first lighted its name was the Sandusky Bay Lighthouse. It 1870 the name was changed to the Marblehead Lighthouse. In 1897 the lighthouse was raised by fifteen feet bringing its height to sixty-five feet.

This early faded photograph of the Sandusky Bay Lighthouse, later known as the Marblehead Lighthouse, indicates primitive surroundings, quite different from what it looks like today.

This 1890s image of the Marblehead Lighthouse shows the new keeper's house, but the tower is still sporting its original lantern room. However, in 1899, the lantern room from the old Erie Land Lighthouse in Erie, PA was removed and installed on the Marblehead Lighthouse, which is the lantern room that is still there to this day.

Early view of the Marblehead Lighthouse before its height was raised and a new lantern room was installed.

Maumee Bay Range Lighthouses

Maumee Bay, Toledo, Ohio

The first lighthouses were built at this location in 1855. The first light was destroyed by ice and the other lights were rebuilt over the years until the three range lights were established. They were officially known as the Maumee Bay Outer Light, Maumee Bay Inner Front Light and the Maumee Bay Outer Front Light. They have also been referred to as the Toledo Crib Range Lights.

Originally the lighthouse keeper had to row between the lighthouses twice a day to maintain the lights, making his job very dangerous in inclement weather. Eventually a dyke was built connecting the lighthouses. The men who served here must all liked living at this lighthouse surrounded by water; they all stayed on for long periods of time. Captain William H. Jennings had one of the longest tenures at an individual lighthouse. Jennings lived here for 49 years until his retirement in 1933. Jennings was replaced by veteran lighthouse keeper Chancie Fitzmorris who had joined the Lighthouse Service in 1903 as a keeper at Sandusky Bay Outer Lighthouse. He served until 1909 when he was transferred to West Sister Island Lighthouse, where he served until arriving at the Maumee Bay Range Lights in 1933. Fitzmorris stayed here until his retirement in 1941. The last keeper was Arthur Bauman, who lived here for slightly over 15 years until the lighthouse was discontinued in December, 1956.

When these lighthouses had outlived their usefulness, everything that was made of iron was removed from the site by a salvage company. The house was offered for free to anyone willing to move it. With no takers, the old keeper's house and everything else that was made of wood at the site was torched and burned to ashes.

One of the earliest of the Maumee Bay Range Lights resembled a silo of sorts. This one was the Middle Range Front Light, which has long ago been lost to the pages of time.

The three Maumee Bay Range Lights are all shown in this image. We have enlarged part of the image in the inset to give a closer view of the Outer Front Light and the ship steaming by the structure. Nothing remains of these three lighthouses that are now among the Ghost Lights of Lake Erie.

The Maumee Middle Range Rear Lighthouse and the Maumee Inner Range Rear Lighthouse were not the typical looking lighthouses. A light shown from the square window at the top of structure. The black bands were painted to help distinguish the structure as a range light in the daytime.

This close-up image shows that the lighthouse keeper of the Maumee Bay Range Lights had a lot of responsibility. Not only did he have to maintain three lighthouses, but the keeper's quarters and other out-buildings had to be maintained. Unlike many of the keepers who lived at lighthouses on islands or the mainland, the keeper here did not have the luxury of cows for fresh milk or chickens for fresh eggs. Getting groceries and other staples to the lighthouse was a major project. The last keeper, Arthur Bauman, lived here for 15 years, with only his mother as a companion and unpaid assistant. All these structures are now gone, lost to the pages of time.

This unique angle shows how dangerous the location of the Maumee Range Lights were as they sat in their exposed locations.

Close-up view in 1945 of the Maumee Bay Outer Front Range Lighthouse. This structure was one of three lighthouses that were the responsibility of the keeper of Maumee Bay Range Lighthouses. This structure was also referred to as the Maumee Bay Inner Range Lighthouse and the Straight Channel Range Lighthouse. Barely seen is lighthouse keeper Arthur Bauman, leaning up against one of the support railings of the lighthouse.

This unique photo shows how the short tower stood up above the pier on a platform and was actually built inside the open framework of the taller tower at the Maumee Bay Range Lights. This type of construction made it unique in lighthouse construction history.

Port Clinton Lighthouses

Port Clinton, Ohio

Built in 1833 to light the entrance to Port Clinton Harbor, the first lighthouse was lit by mirrors with lamps in front of them that were displayed from the mainland side of the tower, facing the harbor. The light came from four lamps that were 26" X 16" and were originally lit by whale oil. The light from the lamps reflected off the mirrors. Later this was changed to eight lamps with bright reflectors placed behind the lamps. The lamps were arranged side by side in the form of a half circle.

The original Port Clinton Lighthouse is shown here after its lantern room was removed and the tower was capped. However, the tower originally had a bird cage style lantern room that was accessed by a wooden circular stairway followed by a ladder going to the lantern room. The keeper's house, with its 20-inch thick stone walls, had a large fireplace in the center that supplied heat to the living quarters. The structure also had a separate enclosed kitchen dining area that had its own fireplace with built-in oven. The tower was torn down in 1899 and the house was torn down shortly thereafter, making it one of the Ghost Lights of Lake Erie.

One often wonders why people settled where they did in those early years of America, which leads to a story that, although is loosely related to the lighthouse, is worthy of mention. In the case of David McRitchie and his wife Jane, it was by chance. Nine days after they were married in Scotland, on June 9, 1832, they sailed for America - the promised-land. During their entire ten weeks voyage to the United States, the seas were heavy with frequent storms and the vessel constantly rocked and rolled on the waves. During this harrowing voyage, someone robbed them of all their money and the couple arrived in America with only ten cents in their pockets. Upon arrival in New York City, the couple was fortunate enough to immediately find employment. They remained in the city for four years, saving their money to move to Chicago, which had been their original destination

However, on their way to Chicago, fate dealt another major blow to their lives. The vessel they were traveling on was shipwrecked and drifted to a sandbar near the Port Clinton Lighthouse. Lighthouse keeper Captain Austin Smith, with the help of a few others, using small boats, rescued them from the sinking vessel. However, the McRitchies had again lost all of their personal possessions, which had been thrown overboard while the crew had tried to keep the ship from sinking.

Lighthouse keeper Smith and his wife offered the despondent couple shelter after the disaster. With little food on hand that first night, their meal consisted simply of some potatoes cooked over a driftwood fire at the lighthouse and flavored with a little salt. The lighthouse family felt sorry for the couple and told them of an abandoned log cabin that they could move into. With some

help from the lighthouse keeper, the couple settled into this primitive structure. They had little choice but vowed to make the best of it. They never made it to Chicago, and eventually the McRitchies became stalwarts of the community and David McRitchie, over time, served in various public positions as Justice of the Peace, Township Clerk, Township Assessor and at the same time, County Auditor and County Treasurer. However, none of this would have been possible if it had not been for the lighthouse keeper saving his life and helping him to settle in the community.

As shipping on the Portage River decreased, the lighthouse was no longer needed. Henry Pope was the last keeper when it was decommissioned in 1843. Although the tower was no longer in use, the old keeper's house was still used as a home and a number of different families occupied it. From 1896 to 1899, Robert Waterfield lived in the house. Waterfield was also the light attendant of the Port Clinton Pier Lighthouse, which had been constructed in 1896.

In 1899 the old tower was torn down. Daniel Finn, who became the second attendant of the Port Clinton Pier Light succeeded Waterfield. In 1900-01, the old stone keeper's house was also torn down and replaced by a new structure.

Eventually a wooden open-frame pyramid tower replaced the short Port Clinton Pierhead Light. The old pierhead lighthouse was sold and eventually moved; it is now on display at the nearby Brands Drydock Marina. The second lighthouse keeper's house also still stands; today it is home to the Garden at the Lighthouse Restaurant.

This was the second lighthouse to serve Port Clinton. The wooden structure, officially known as the Port Clinton Pier Light, stood on the west pier at the entrance to the Portage River. Sometimes the lighthouse was referred to as the Portage River Entrance Light. When this image was taken, the lighthouse was in full use. The round building to the right was used as an oil storage shed. Since there were no living facilities at this light, a keeper's house was constructed on the mainland. (Lighthouse Digest *archives.*)

This structure served as the boat house for the Port Clinton Lighthouse Station. The man standing in the sailboat appears to be the lighthouse keeper. The old boathouse stood for many years, being used by the City of Port Clinton as a storage building at a local baseball field. It was demolished in 2010. (Lighthouse Digest *archives.*)

125

Light House, Port Clinton, Ohio.

Apparently the lighthouse keeper was enjoying the beautiful day as this small excursion boat with its many flags sailed past the lighthouse in this vintage post card scene. After the structure was no longer needed, it was sold to Clair and Eddie Jeremy for $1.00. In the late 1970s, Brands Drydock Marina purchased the land and they have continued to maintain the historic structure, which still stands today. (Lighthouse Digest *archives.*)

The waters were calm at the time this image of the Port Clinton Lighthouse was taken. (Lighthouse Digest *archives.*)

Sandusky Bay Lighthouses

Sandusky, Ohio

As with so much of our nation's lighthouse history, the history, stories and memories as well as the photographs of the lighthouse keepers of the various lighthouses in Sandusky have been elusive. With the exception of the Cedar Point Lighthouse, mentioned in a previous chapter and some nondescript modern aids to navigation, all of the historic lighthouses of Sandusky have been lost to the pages of time.

Sandusky's lighthouse history dates back to 1823, when early records indicate a lighthouse here with 13 lamps and 13 reflectors was established. By 1895 reports indicate the cribs were sunk in the channel to support the foundations for two lighthouses. It was later reported in 1926 that both of these lighthouses were deliberately burned to make way for new modern structures, which were also eventually replaced by cylindrical steel towers. Since there were so many lighthouses built in Sandusky Bay, the history of the station can be confusing and is often intertwined, especially in old newspaper stories.

Charles C. Sellman, who arrived as the keeper of Sandusky Bay Outer Lighthouse in January 1910, after short stints at the Ashtabula Lighthouse in Ohio and the Buffalo Breakwater Lighthouse in New York, never served his full potential at the lighthouse. He died on the job in March, 1917, at the young age of 45, leaving behind a wife and two daughters, Mae and Clara. Being a very religious man, he had been very active in the First Baptist Church of Sandusky.

This early Sandusky Bay West Pier Lighthouse was a lantern atop a large pole that protruded from a small wooden structure. (Lighthouse Digest *archives.*)

The Sandusky Bay Inner Range Rear Lighthouse is shown here in 1913. Although there were simple accommodations at the structure for emergencies, the lighthouse keeper for this beacon lived on the mainland. The lighthouse was destroyed by a controlled fire in 1926 to make room for a modern structure. (Lighthouse Digest *archives.*)

The Sandusky Bay Rear Range Lighthouse as it appeared when it was painted a color other than white. (Lighthouse Digest *archives.*)

The workmen on the scow at the wharf with supplies to build the Sandusky Bay Front Range Lighthouse took a moment to pose for this historic photograph. (Lighthouse Digest *archives.*)

The Sandusky Bay Front Range Lighthouse was built in 1895. When this photo was taken, with the two keepers standing on the crib, the structure was painted white. Since some of the extra architectural extras had not yet been added, this photo may have been taken shortly after the structure was completed. (Lighthouse Digest *archives.*)

The Sandusky Bay Outer Range Front Lighthouse. Notice the lighthouse keeper's wife in her long dress posing for this photograph. (U.S. Coast Guard photo, Lighthouse Digest *archives.)*

By the time this image was taken of the Sandusky Bay Front Range Lighthouse, shutters had been added and the structure had a more warm feeling to it. (Lighthouse Digest *archives.*)

Shown on the front deck of the Sandusky Bay Inner Front Range Lighthouse is lighthouse keeper Frank Ritter with three of his children. The lady may have been his wife. Ritter became the lighthouse keeper here in March of 1893 and served here until his retirement in January of 1929. Although the nearby Cedar Point Lighthouse, also in Sandusky, had been discontinued, Ritter also managed the additional duties at the old lighthouse and all the other aids to navigation in the area from 1904 until 1909. (Photograph courtesy Sandusky Library Follett House Museum Archives.)

Lighthouses like homes often changed in appearance as shown in this image when the Sandusky Bay Front Range Lighthouse was painted a color other than white. (Lighthouse Digest *archives.*)

This square structure was the Sandusky Bay Range Main Beacon. Completed in 1879, the square structure was rather nondescript and looked somewhat like a military blockhouse. However, its white picket fence gave it a certain tone of distinction. Sadly, the structure no longer stands. (Lighthouse Digest *archives.*)

This duplex served as the on-shore residence of the keepers of the Sandusky Bay Lighthouses. Here the families of the lighthouse keepers lived, played and talked about the days of the great sailing ships of yesteryear. (Lighthouse Digest *archives.*)

Although this image is somewhat faded with age, it shows two keeper's in the lighthouse dory probably on their way to one of the Sandusky Bay Pier Lighthouses. The pennant flying from the bow of the dory is the official flag of the Bureau of Lighthouses, more commonly known as the United States Lighthouse Service. (Lighthouse Digest *archives.*)

This beacon was once one of the Sandusky Bay Range Lights. This structure stood until the mid 1990s when it was replaced by a modern nondescript cylindrical stove pipe style structure. (U.S. Coast Guard photo, Lighthouse Digest *archives.)*

Turtle Island Lighthouse

Harborview, Ohio

The tiny Turtle Island, with its storied history, is located in Lake Erie near the Michigan and Ohio state line, northeast of the mouth of the Maumee River.

Many stories about the early use of the island are mixed with folklore and fact, making it sometimes difficult to distinguish one from the other. However, the island was originally used by Native Americans who visited the island to collect seagull eggs. The island was named in honor of Chief Little Turtle of the Miami Tribe who was one of the most noted military leaders of his time.

All throughout the 1700s and ending with the conclusion of the War of 1812, Turtle Island played a significant role as a military outpost. But it wasn't until the beginning of commercial shipping on the Great Lakes that the government realized a need for a light-

The second structure to be called the Turtle Island Lighthouse was discontinued in 1904. It is shown here in its prime when it was an active lighthouse station. (National Archives photograph.)

133

house here to mark the entrance to Toledo Harbor.

By 1831 the government built the first lighthouse here and also spent $2,000 to help shore up the island, which was beginning to shrink in size from erosion. The structure consisted of a tower built of yellow square brick and stone, attached to a wooden keeper's house.

Over the years the island continued to suffer from erosion and at one point the nearly seven acre island and was reduced to less than one acre. However, the government eventually spent enough money building erosion control systems and walls that the shrinkage stopped. It has been stated that the government, between 1831 and 1903 spent over one million dollars in erosion controls on the island. However, government attempts to control the erosion came to a halt when the lighthouse was discontinued and the island and the lighthouse were sold into private ownership.

The first early keepers of the lighthouse must not have found the station to the best of their liking. William Wilson arrived in April of 1832 and quit the following month. Bernard Cass then became the keeper, but he served less than one year and resigned in March of 1833.

The job then went to Samuel Choate, a military veteran who had served gallantly in the War of 1812, who assumed the position of

This is all that remains today of the Turtle Island Lighthouse. In modern times, there have been some efforts to bring life back to the island. However, because of a combination of financial problems, legal setbacks and the harsh elements, all have been unsuccessful. (Photograph courtesy Bob and Sandra Shanklin, "The Lighthouse People.")

lighthouse keeper on March 11, 1833. However, he also did not last long on the job. When it was noticed that a light was not shining from the tower, a local man went to investigate. He found a weeping wife with two small children. Lighthouse keeper Choate, 67, had died of cholera and had been buried on the island by his son, Seth, who himself died a couple of days later, also of cholera. The man then brought the keeper's wife, two surviving children and the body of the son back to the mainland. A few days later, one of the two children, a girl, also died of cholera.

Apparently, Benjamin Woodruff, who was appointed to replace Choate as the lighthouse keeper, had no intentions of going to the island where he might have become infected by the germs from the cholera outbreak; he never even reported for duty.

The lighthouse continued to serve well over the next years with a number of differ-

ent keepers. However, in the time leading up to and during the Civil War, there was no money allotted for repairs and maintenance to the lighthouse and it soon fell into a state of disrepair. The government decided to build a new brick lighthouse at the site, which was completed and put into service in September 1866. Andrew Harrison, who had arrived at Turtle Island in 1861, was the last keeper to serve at the old lighthouse and the first to serve at the new lighthouse. He stayed until August of 1867 when he resigned.

Harrison's replacement was Nathan W. Edson who served until he died on the job. Edson's death is a tragic reminder of the dangers of lighthouse life in those early years on Lake Erie. It was early in March of 1869 when the lighthouse keeper at nearby West Sister Island Lighthouse, John Edson, had died. John Edson's son-in-law, Martin Goulden, took the West Sister Island Lighthouse boat and launched it in an effort to go to Toledo to get a coffin. However, Goulden got caught in a typical Lake Erie March blizzard. Somehow, he was able to land the boat at Turtle Island, where he sought refuge with the lighthouse keeper and his family. The following day, keeper Nathan Edson decided to assist Goulden, and the two men launched the boat for another attempted trip to Toledo for the coffin. However, the stormy waters of Lake Erie had not yet subsided from the previous day's storm. The water was extremely choppy and rogue waves came from different directions. One of those waves hit the small boat so hard that the vessel broke into pieces. Although the two men were able to cling to the wreckage for a short time, the situation was hopeless. Hypothermia soon set in and within a very short time both men died.

It is unclear whether West Sister Island Lighthouse keeper John Edson and Turtle Island Lighthouse keeper Nathan Edson were related. However, they probably were. It was not uncommon for a son to follow in his father's footsteps and become a lighthouse keeper, and quite often brothers and cousins from the same family would become lighthouse keepers. Whatever the case, it was a tragic week for the families at the two Lake Erie lighthouses.

Nathan Edson was replaced as the lighthouse keeper at Turtle Island by his wife, Ann, who held the job until September 1872 when she left the island.

The last keeper, William Haynes, served at Turtle Island Lighthouse slightly over an amazing 29 years, from March, 1875 to May 15, 1904 when the lighthouse was discontinued. Haynes was then transferred to Monroe Lighthouse in Monroe, Michigan.

When the Turtle Island Lighthouse was discontinued, it was replaced by the Toledo Harbor Lighthouse which was built about 3½ miles away. Shortly thereafter, the Turtle Island Lighthouse and the island was put up for auction and sold into private ownership. Over the years, ownership has changed several times, but the elements and vandals were too much for the private owners who were not located at the site.

The vandals were the first to attack the lighthouse, stealing everything they could and damaging what they felt like. The cause of its eventual demise is dispute by historians. However, whether the final blow came to the lighthouse as a result of a tornado and high winds in 1965, or if it was the elements that finally took their toll, the results were the same. Today, other than the remnants of the tower, which is minus its lantern room, very little is left of the once proud Turtle Island Lighthouse, which is now one of the Ghost Lights of Lake Erie.

Vermilion Lighthouses

Vermilion, Ohio

Although a lighthouse structure stands today in Vermilion, it is not a real lighthouse, but a replica, constructed in 1991 to replicate the 1877 lighthouse. Although the 1877 Vermilion Lighthouse is long gone, interestingly, it still stands today, as another lighthouse, at a much different location. It is included in this book, because, in fact, the real Vermilion Lighthouse, in all actuality, no longer exists as the Vermilion Lighthouse.

The first Vermilion Lighthouse was built in 1846 and was a wooden tower that was rebuilt in 1859. When the old wooden tower had aged beyond repair, a new structure that had been fabricated in Buffalo, New York

The original 1846 Vermilion Lighthouse is shown here after it was renovated in 1859. By 1878 it had been replaced and lost to the pages of time. (National Archives photograph.)

was transported in sections by barge to Vermilion where in 1877 it was erected at the end of a 400-foot pier.

A number of the early keepers of the Vermillion Lighthouse did not stay long. The first keeper, William B. Andrews, resigned in July 1851. He was replaced by James Anderson, who also resigned after serving only nine months on the job. The job was then offered to Theodore King, who after thinking about it for a few days, declined the offer. The third keeper at Vermilion was Charles P. Judson, who served for a little less than two years until April 1854 when he also resigned.

The next two keepers served longer stints at Vermilion, but they were both removed from their jobs. O.H. Allen, who had become keeper in 1854, lasted for seven years when he was removed, probably for political reasons. William B. Andrews served as the keeper from 1861 to 1868, when he was also removed. During part of that time, from 1863 to 1868, he had an assistant named George E. Andrews, who was most likely a relative. Amazingly, the next keeper, Burton Parsons, in 1873 was also removed from the job after serving four years. The next two keepers, Charles B. Miles and Harris Miles, both died on the job; Charles died in 1879 and Harris died in 1901. After 1901, things seem to stabilize themselves at Vermilion and remained calm until the lighthouse was discontinued in 1920.

As the lighthouse era began to change through modernization and automation, the Vermillion Lighthouse was automated and its keepers were removed. At that time the keeper's house, located on shore, was sold. It must have been a sad day when the last keeper, Joseph Wetzler, had to move out of the keeper's house and look for new employment. The care of the lighthouse, although it was automated, was then assigned to the keeper of the Lorain Lighthouse.

Ernest H. Wakefield, in his book *The Lighthouse That Wanted To Stay Lit,* recounted the final days of the Vermilion Lighthouse. It was in the summer of 1929 when teenage brothers, Theodore and Ernest Wakefield, while playing on the pier, noticed that the lighthouse was leaning, and went home and informed their father, Commodore Frederick Wakefield. After going to inspect the site for himself, the Commodore immediately notified the district office of the Lighthouse Service in Cleveland that the Vermilion Lighthouse was about to topple over into the water. Within a week, a U. S. Corps of Engineers steam tug, along with a derrick-bearing barge and a scow, arrived in the harbor to remove the lighthouse. The Commodore tried to buy the lighthouse and have it installed on his property, but his request was denied.

The Vermilion Lighthouse was disassembled and placed aboard the barge *Erie* and then transported to Buffalo, New York, where it remained in storage for a number of years. Slightly altered, in 1935 the tower was then brought to a location near Cape Vincent, New York where it became the East Charity Shoal Lighthouse on Lake Ontario near the entrance to the St. Lawrence River.

Interestingly, in later years, it was one of Commodore Wakefield's sons, Ted, who spearheaded the move to build a replica of the Vermilion Lighthouse that stands in Vermilion today.

The 1877 Vermilion Lighthouse as it appeared in 1908 when light-house keeper John H. Burns maintained a well kept station. As was typical during the daylight hours, the curtains were drawn on the lantern room to protect the valuable Fresnel lens from the harmful rays of the sun. The Fresnel lens had originally been transported by train from Cleveland to Vermilion when it was installed in the tower in 1877. The round structure shown next to the lighthouse was the oil storage shed. (Lighthouse Digest *archives.*)

This vintage real photo post card shows a vessel named the EDNA B. going past the Vermilion Lighthouse at full speed. Exactly what was happening here is unclear, but there is a cameraman sitting in the back of the vessel. The other people in the boat are dressed in white and could have been surf-men from the United States Life-Saving Service, which became the Coast Guard in 1915. (Lighthouse Digest *archives.*)

Olin W. Stevens, shown here on the right, was the 1st Assistant keeper at Vermilion Lighthouse from 1919 to 1920. He was promoted to keeper at the Lorain Lighthouse and from there he went on to serve at the Tibbetts Point Lighthouse in New York. He finished his lighthouse career at the Oswego Harbor West Pierhead Lighthouse, also in New York, where he retired in 1951. The other person in this 1942 photograph is not identified. In 1939 when the U.S. Lighthouse Service was dissolved and merged into the Coast Guard, the lighthouse keepers were given the choice of remaining on as civilian lighthouse keepers or joining the Coast Guard. Stevens chose the Coast Guard. (Photograph courtesy Olin M. Stevens.)

Much to the dismay and disappointment of the citizens of Vermilion, this steel skeleton tower with a beacon on top replaced the Vermillion Lighthouse in 1930. (Lighthouse Digest *archives.*)

The East Charity Shoal Lighthouse, located on Lake Ontario near the entrance to the St. Lawrence Seaway off the coast of Cape Vincent, New York, was once the Vermilion Lighthouse. It is the only lighthouse structure on the Great Lakes to have stood on guard on two different lakes. In 1877 the lighthouse was transported from Buffalo, New York by barge and erected in Vermilion, Ohio. In 1929, when it was removed from Vermilion, Ohio, it was again transported by barge back to Buffalo, New York where it remained in storage at the Lighthouse Depot. In 1935 it was again transported from Buffalo, New York, but this time to its new home on Lake Ontario, where it was erected with some modifications. East Charity Shoals Lighthouse was never a manned lighthouse and was always automated. It was eventually declared excess property by the government, which sold the lighthouse in August 2009 to a private individual from Dallas, Texas. (*Lighthouse Digest* archives.)

West Sister Island Lighthouses

Maumee Bay, Ohio

Although there is a lighthouse tower still standing on West Sister Island, it is so dramatically different from what was once there that the West Sister Island Lighthouse Station, for all practical purposes, is one of the Ghost Lights of Lake Erie.

American history buffs, especially those who study Great Lakes and Lake Erie history, will recall the famous message sent from near here in the War of 1812, more so than they will know about the lighthouse. In a dispatch sent to General William Henry Harrison, Commodore Oliver Perry, who had just defeated the British, penned the following, "We have met the enemy and they are ours." The message was datelined, "Off West Sister Island."

As the communities on the Lake Erie began to grow, the government felt it was necessary to build a lighthouse on the west side of the island to mark the west end of the South Passage through the lake's Bass Islands. The first keeper assigned here in October of 1847 was Alexander Cromwell, who was only here for one month when he was transferred to Turtle Island Lighthouse. He was followed by Gideon Kelsey who stayed for three years.

Although the lighthouse keepers had all the comforts of a house on the mainland and the lighthouse tenders delivered supplies when the weather permitted, in most of the winter months they were cut off from the mainland.

It was reported that Harrison Haynes, who was the keeper from April of 1871 to May of

The earliest known image of the West Sister Island Lighthouse shows the station to be a primitive outpost. The tower had a bird cage style lantern room. (Lighthouse Digest *archives.*)

West Sister Island Lighthouse with the original keepers houses as it appeared in 1867 when a new lantern room was installed on the tower and an enclosed entryway building was built. (National Archives photograph.)

1885, decided to raise some turkeys for extra income. Just before Thanksgiving one year, he killed and dressed 75 turkeys that were to be picked up and sold on the mainland. However, when the boat that was going to pick up the turkeys could not reach the island because of the weather conditions, he was stuck with all the turkeys. His daughter reported that the family ate turkey for weeks thereafter.

Gladys McMeans, who wrote the book *My Island Home* about her time on the island when her father Horace Curd was the lighthouse keeper from April 1908 to November 1909, provided an excellent look at what it was like on the island for a lighthouse family.

Curd, who had served on Admiral Sampson's flagship during the Spanish America War, came to West Sister Island Lighthouse with some past lighthouse experience. He had previously served as a second assistant keeper and 1st assistant keeper at the Presque Isle Pierhead Lighthouse in Pennsylvania, and as the keeper at Sunken Rock Lighthouse in New York.

McMeans wrote that her family didn't mind the isolation, mainly because the family got along so well together. They played lots of board games, were home-schooled by their parents, and had a collection of animals including a horse, chickens, three goats, three geese, two cows, two cats and even a pair of donkeys. The home was comfortable and the children helped with the cooking and baking.

However, keeper Curd and his wife soon realized that island life was not in the best interest of raising a family. The children were not in school, trips to the mainland were too frequent and long, and in some instances dangerous, and he wanted to raise his family among other people. He resigned the prestigious job of being a lighthouse keeper and bought a farm on the mainland.

Chancie Fitzmorris was the next person to serve as the keeper at West Sister Island and he stayed there until 1933 when he was transferred to Maumee Bay where he served until his retirement in 1941, after serving an amazing 38 years as a lighthouse keeper. However, while stationed at West Sister

West Sister Island Lighthouse as it appeared in 1904 with a new and larger keeper's house that was built in 1867/68. The round structure was the oil storage building. (U.S. Coast Guard photo, Lighthouse Digest *archives.)*

Island Lighthouse, he was injured when he was attacked by a bull on March 31, 1919. Fitzmorris, in believing that a lighthouse keeper is always on duty, filed a claim for his injuries and medical expenses. However, the government did not agree and ruled "At the time of his injury the keeper was engaged in his usual routine chores. The animal which inflicted the injury was the personal property of the claimant. In view of the foregoing facts it is held that the claimant was engaged on his own personal business and the injury was not sustained while in the performance of duty for the Government."

The last lighthouse keeper to serve on the island was George B. Gampher, who lived on the island with his mother. During their 13 years on the island, they were credited with saving a number of lives of many stranded fishermen and survivors of shipwrecks. Gampher left the island in 1937 when the lighthouse was automated and the buildings were abandoned.

In 1938, by presidential proclamation, the island became a wildlife refuge and was declared off limits to the public. However, during World War II, the military could have cared less about the protected wildlife. They used the island for artillery practice. Shortly after the conclusion of the war, what was left of the structures was demolished and the lantern room was removed from the lighthouse.

When Gladys McMeans returned to the island in 1994, for the first time since she had left in 1909, she was disappointed in what she saw. Nearly everything of what she remembered was gone. Her family even had difficulty in locating the foundations of the keeper's house and other buildings which had all been overgrown with trees and brush. The biggest disgrace was that the lighthouse had been decapitated, which, other than being torn down, is the worst thing that can be done to an historic lighthouse. She suggested to the wildlife officials that accompanied her that the least they could do is clear the brush out around the foundation of the keeper's house and install a fence around it with an interpretative sign. They said they would take her recommendation under consideration; however, they probably never really considered it.

West Sister Island Lighthouse from the time Gladys McMeans lived there as a young child in the early 1900s. It was a well maintained station with beautiful manicured grounds. (Lighthouse Digest *archives.*)

West Sister Island Lighthouse as it appeared in 1936 after the lantern room was removed from the tower and the keeper's house was still standing. In 1945, what was left of the keeper's house, along with the oil storage building, barn, boathouse, chicken house, carpenter shop, children's play house and school room, were all demolished. (U.S. Coast Guard photo, Lighthouse Digest *archives.*)

The trees and brush have obliterated where the keeper's house at West Sister Island Lighthouse once stood. The decapitated lighthouse is all that remains of the historic station where lighthouse keepers and their families once served so faithfully and in some cases, in great peril, in the duty of keeping the waterway safe for others. (Photograph courtesy Bob and Sandra Shanklin, "The Lighthouse People.")

Presque Isle Lighthouses

Erie, Pennsylvania

Today, Erie, Pennsylvania is home to three lighthouses that are all popular tourist attractions. But in the pages of time, things were once much different than they are today. The history of Erie's lighthouses is often confusing, and because of the similarity in names and name changes, the history of these lighthouses has sometimes been mistakenly interwoven. To add to the confusion, many of Pennsylvania's other lighthouses that were located on the Delaware River, on the other side of the state, no longer stand. One of those, the original Schooner Ledge Rear Range Lighthouse, located two miles south of Chester, Pennsylvania was moved to Wisconsin where it became the new Michigan Island Lighthouse.

Additionally, the lighthouses of Erie might have been listed as being in a state other than Pennsylvania, if it were not for an agreement reached in the late 1700s, when New York, Massachusetts, and even Connecticut gave up their claims to this area, which then allowed the State of Pennsylvania to have a port on Lake Erie.

Known as the Presque Isle Lighthouse, the first tower to be built here was back in 1818. By 1851 the old tower was in bad shape, and in an effort to save the tower metal bands were placed around the tower. Eventually the old tower was torn down and a new tower was built and completed in 1858. However, after a few short years the tower shown here began to settle, and it was discovered that the heavy structure was sitting on a base of quicksand that was hidden well below the surface. The tower was dismantled in 1866 in favor of a rebuilding at a new site a short distance away.

Completed in 1867, this became the third Presque Isle Lighthouse. However, its usefulness was questioned when a new, nearby, Presque Isle Lighthouse was built in 1873. At that time, this tower was discontinued and its lantern room and lens were removed. The tower became known as the old Erie Land Light and the government sold the property and the lighthouse. However, after local mariners protested, the lighthouse was again put back into service and in 1885 its lantern room and lens were replaced.

The Erie Land Light continued in service until the government again decided the lighthouse was no longer needed and it was discontinued for the second time, this time for good. In 1901, the lens and lantern room were removed, moved and installed at the Marblehead Lighthouse in Ohio. For the next 100 years, the lighthouse stood without a lantern room.

By this time the locals referred to the old structure simply as "The Land Light."

In 1934, the lighthouse was given to the City of Erie. In 1989, a wooden replica of the lantern room was installed atop the lighthouse. The lighthouse was threatened again in 2003 when a severe storm heavily damaged the lantern room but did not damage the tower.

As part of a $400,000 restoration project, in 2004 a new lantern room was fabricated and installed atop the Erie Land Light and an elaborate ceremony was held to rededicate the lighthouse. (Lighthouse Digest *archives.*)

Thanks to the efforts of dedicated preservationists, such as Mrs. Kitty Felion and many others, the restored Erie Land Lighthouse did not become one of the Ghost Lights of Lake Erie. (Lighthouse Digest *archives.*)

Early image of the first Erie North Pierhead Light. Apparently this tower was still standing in 1910 when this postcard was postmarked. On the back was written. "This is where the whole bunch goes every Sunday from the Presque Isle Club." (Lighthouse Digest *archives.*)

This rare image of an early Erie Pierhead Light shows two other tall structures on or close to the pier. The furthest one appears to be another pier light and another structure appears to be a lookout tower of some kind. (Lighthouse Digest *archives.*)

This vintage postcard image of the Erie North Pierhead Lighthouse shows when the pier was extended and the lighthouse was moved and the tower was a wooden frame structure. Unfortunately, the artist used some artistic license in designing the card. The ore carrier and other ship passing by appear to be toy ships — or the people are twenty feet tall. In real life, vessels of this size would have dwarfed the lighthouses. (Lighthouse Digest *archives.*)

Early image of Erie North Pierhead Lighthouse when the tower was made of wood. The structure in the distance is the fog bell tower. The Erie Pierhead Lighthouse was eventually encased in metal and was painted one color. Today it is painted white with a black band in the middle. (Lighthouse Digest *archives.*)

This is the structure that replaced the earlier lighthouse that became known as the Erie Land Lighthouse and was shown previously. Thousands of people visit the Presque Isle State Park in Erie to view the Presque Isle Lighthouse. However, they won't see a tower that looks like this, which is much shorter than the tower that is there now. This image of the lighthouse was taken in 1885 before the lighthouse was raised in 1896. The completion of a road to the lighthouse also brought more visitors to the station, much to the dismay of lighthouse keeper Andrew Shaw Jr. He had enjoyed the quiet life at the lighthouse. Rather than put up with all the visitors, after being keeper for 26 years, he took an early retirement in 1927. (U.S. Coast Guard photo, Lighthouse Digest *archives.)*

The Presque Isle Lighthouse as it appeared in 1911 showing a much taller tower than was previously there and shown in the previous photo. The lighthouse looks relatively the same today. (*U.S. Coast Guard photo,* Lighthouse Digest *archives.*)

The Presque Isle Fog Bell Tower as it appeared in 1911. Structures like this were not uncommon on Lake Erie. (*U.S. Coast Guard photo,* Lighthouse Digest *archives.*)

August Gramer

Lighthouse Keeper

A book about the lighthouses of Lake Erie would not be complete without mention of August "Gus," Gramer, whose sixteen year, on-again, off-again, career with the United States Light House Establishment was a challenge for his superiors.

Gramer's maritime career started at the age of 15 when he joined the crew of a whaling vessel. During his whaling years, he sailed in the waters of the Arctic, the Antarctic and the South Pacific. It was on one such adventure in the South Pacific that the vessel he was on was shipwrecked. He and his fellow crewmembers sought refuge on an island that was inhabited by savages, and he and the crew nearly lost their lives. Fortunately, he and others were rescued, but that ended his career on whaling vessels.

However, he was not done with the sea and joined the United States Navy where he served for the next 20 years. By 1895 he had apparently had enough of Navy life and became an employee of the United States Light House Board, which was also known as the United States Lighthouse Establishment.

His first assignment in September of 1893 was lightship duty, and he was assigned to the *Lime Kiln Crossing Light Vessel* which served in the waters off Monroe, Michigan in the Detroit River. Light Vessels, or lightships as they were more commonly called, were a stationary vessel that was anchored in an area

Lighthouse keeper August Gramer as taken from an old newspaper clipping. A strong-willed keeper credited with saving lives, his lighthouse career came to a strange conclusion.

where it was either impossible or too expensive to build a lighthouse. Lightships were never allowed to leave their location, regardless of the weather conditions. Lightship duty was considered the most dangerous duty of all government lighthouse work.

Being stationed on a stationary vessel that never went anywhere must have been quite a change for Gramer who was used to traveling the world. However, he remained on lightship duty until August, 22, 1895 when he accepted the position of lighthouse keeper at the Ecorse Range Lighthouse. However, in 1898, he took a leave of absence to rejoin the Navy and fight in the Spanish America War. Although the war lasted less than a year, Gramer extended his leave of absence from the lighthouse for eight years until he returned as the keeper of the light in November, 1906. During that time his wife and daughter had assumed the position as keeper of the light.

In May, 1907 Gramer was transferred to the Monroe Lighthouse where he served a little less that a year before being transferred in April of 1908 to the Toledo Harbor Lighthouse in Ohio, an appointment he would later regret.

Prior to his arrival in Toledo, Gramer had distinguished himself as a lighthouse keeper with a number of heroic rescues, and he had received citations for his efficiency. He even invented a grappling hook that could be used in locating the bodies of drowned victims. Upon his arrival in Toledo, he donated a set of his hooks to the city that subsequently used them for many years.

However, from nearly the day Gramer arrived at Toledo Harbor Lighthouse, the assistant keepers of the lighthouse apparently, for one reason or another, did not always see eye to eye with him. First assistant keeper Edward Jennings resigned on September 3,

1908, and a few days later, on September 6, 1908, 2nd assistant keeper Horace Shaddock also resigned. Then, 2nd assistant keeper Delaney resigned on February 28, 1909, and 1st assistant keeper C. Gage transferred out the same day. Assistant keeper Frank Bell, who arrived on March 18, 1909, only stayed three months and resigned on June 20, 1909.

At some point, one of the assistant keepers sent a letter to government officials complaining of Gramer's so-called abrasive behavior and contempt for regulations and procedures. Whether the accusations were true or not, Roscoe House, the Superintendent of the Tenth Lighthouse District, went out to the lighthouse to investigate. Gramer, said to be a man who was used to being in charge, was apparently infuriated by the Superintendent's confrontational visit and told him to "go to hell." Obviously, that

For a number of years, August "Gus" Gramer served on the Lime Kiln Crossing Lightship. This rare photo shows the Lime Kiln Crossing North Lightship, the Lime Kiln Crossing South Lightship and the Ballard Reef Lightship. All the vessels served at different locations in the Detroit River. There are no longer any lightships on duty in the United States. Less than a dozen of them survive and a few of them are now museums. (Photograph courtesy Jim Claflin collection.)

was not the way to talk to a Lighthouse Superintendent.

With the blessing of the Light House Board, Superintendent House later notified Gramer in writing to appear at an official hearing where he would have a chance to give his side of the story or face dismissal. Gramer not only did not show up at the hearing, he also did not bother to send a letter to defend himself or explain why he couldn't show up at the hearing. The Light House Board found him guilty of insubordination and fired him.

Since there was no lighthouse tender available at the time, Lighthouse Superintendent House hired a local boat to take him out to the lighthouse. Upon his arrival, he informed Gramer that he had been dismissed and he was ordered to take his personal possessions and leave the lighthouse. Gramer refused.

The only alternative for Superintendent House was to return to the mainland and get help to remove Gramer from the lighthouse. His reinforcements consisted of two police detectives and the local United States Marshal.

By this time word had spread throughout the community and a small crowd of people and newspaper reporters had gathered at the dock to watch the armed party leave and head out to the lighthouse. As much as some of the reporters begged to come along, they were advised that it might be too dangerous and their requests were denied.

Upon seeing the armed landing party arrive at the lighthouse, Gramer realized his time was up and he had no choice but to leave peacefully. Obviously he felt this was no way to treat a man who had served his country in so many distinguished ways, but he also must have known he had overstepped his bounds. However, needless to say, he was not happy about it.

When the boat reached the mainland and as the group disembarked from the boat, Gramer got in the last word. As he started to walk away, and within earshot of the reporters, he turned and shouted, "You guys can't fire me – I quit." And so, August "Gus" Gramer, one of the colorful lighthouse keepers of Lake Erie, disappeared into the pages of lighthouse history. One month later, Charles E. Chapman was appointed the lighthouse keeper at the Toledo Harbor Lighthouse and he served there for approximately eight years, leaving the job in 1917.

August Gramer died at his Toledo home in 1933 and was buried at the Memorial Park Cemetery.

(Research courtesy of Kathy Covert Warnes.)

The Toledo Harbor Lighthouse, Ohio, where Augustus "Gus" Gramer's lighthouse career came to an abrupt end. The lighthouse is now under the care of the very capable and active Toledo Harbor Lighthouse Preservation Society.
(Lighthouse Digest *archives.*)

From the Dusty Pages of Time

Since the 1800s, the image of a lighthouse has been used to promote products by helping to draw attention to the actual advertisement with a subliminal message indicating, "Do business with us; we are a rock solid company" or "like a lighthouse, you can trust your business to us."

Throughout modern times, many businesses have also used the word lighthouse in their name, such as the Lighthouse Soap Company, which made everything from Lighthouse Cleanser to Lighthouse Wash Soap. For many years the National Grocer Company produced Light House Coffee, Light House Peanut Butter and Light House Rolled Oats. If they can be found, the containers for many of those old products have become highly sought-after collectibles.

Shown here is a vintage 1800s advertisement for the C & B Line. which stands for The Cleveland & Buffalo Transit Company that featured a lighthouse in their advertisement.

This advertisement promotes two of their new steamers, "City of Buffalo," that was launched in 1896, and "City of Erie" that made its debut in 1898.

A combination of railroad competition, the growth of automobile use by the public and the Great Depression ate away at the profitability of the great passenger excursion

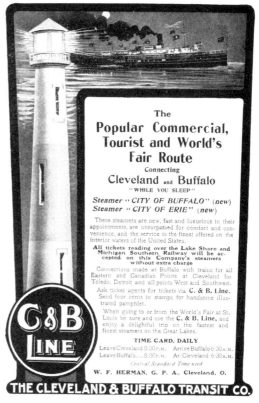

ships on Lake Erie and the other Great Lakes pushed the Cleveland and Buffalo Transit Company into bankruptcy in 1939. The *City of Buffalo* was destroyed by a fire in 1938 and in 1939 the *City of Erie* was sold for salvage. However, the company was reorganized in 1943 as a trucking company.

161

1900s image of the City of Erie one of the great passenger excursion boats that once operated daily in the waters of Lake Erie between Cleveland, Ohio and Buffalo, New York. (Lighthouse Digest *archives.*)

This neat vintage post card of a lighthouse facsimile still stands today, although with a slightly different look, as part of the floral exhibits in Washington Park in Sandusky, Ohio.

This historic image of the SS Edmund Fitzgerald, *going past the Toledo Harbor Lighthouse as it was leaving the Port of Toledo in October 1975, was taken by Dan Grzelak and Ted Golkiewicz as they were perch fishing near the Toledo Harbor Lighthouse. Little could they have known at the time, that in a matter of days, in a violent storm, the great ship would sink with the loss of its entire crew, approximately 15 miles northwest of Michigan's Whitefish Point Lighthouse. Although there have literally been hundreds and hundreds of shipwrecks on the Great Lakes, sadly, the sinking of the* SS Edmund Fitzgerald *is the most notable shipping disaster on the Great Lakes. The disaster was immortalized in Gordon Lightfoot's 1976 hit song, "The Wreck of the Edmund Fitzgerald."*

United States Life Saving Service

The United States Life Saving Service originally started as a private and volunteer organization to help rescue the lives of people from shipwrecks. The federal government got involved in 1848 by operating some stations under the control of the Revenue Cutter Service, which was originally the Revenue Marine Service.

In 1878 the federal government officially created the United States Life Saving Service as a separate entity. Depending on the area that the stations were built, and the duties assigned, they were called by various names; life-saving stations, life boat stations or harbor of refuge stations. Among those that were built on Lake Erie were those in Ohio at Fairport, Cleveland, Sandusky, and Vermilion, at Buffalo, New York and at Presque Isle in Erie, Pennsylvania. The Life Saving Service was often referred to as the sister organization of the Lighthouse Service and many Life Saving Stations were located near lighthouses.

The motto of the surfmen whose job it was to rescue victims of shipwrecks was, "You have to go out, but you don't have to come back." This meant that they were required to save lives, even if meant giving up their own.

In 1915 the United States Life Saving Service and the United States Revenue Cutter Service were merged to form the United States Coast Guard. Although some of our nation's Life Saving Service stations have been saved, most of them no longer stand, having been lost to the pages of time.

The Life Boat

Some life saving stations had rails and ramps down to the water while others used a ramp with rollers, as shown here, to launch the rescue boat. (Lighthouse Digest archives.)

This image of the Cleveland Ohio Life Saving Service Station with the Cleveland West Pier Lighthouse shows a well maintained station. (Lighthouse Digest *archives.*)

Some of the surfmen at the Presque Isle Life Saving Station in Erie, Pennsylvania take a break in their training to pose for this photograph. The life saving station is directly behind them. (Lighthouse Digest *archives.*)

Various types of life boats were used and transported in various ways to and from the water. Although most stations could launch the rescue boat right from the station and into the water, some had to be hauled by horse drawn cart or by brut human strength. (Lighthouse Digest *archives.*)

This may have been a celebration of the opening of the Marblehead (Sandusky) Life Saving Station in 1876 or the christening of a new rescue boat. Whatever the case, a large number of people were on hand for the event. (Photograph courtesy Ohio Historical Society.)

Because Buffalo was such a busy harbor, in 1877 the United States Life Saving Service built a life saving station in Buffalo. In 1915 the U.S. Revenue Cutter Service and the U.S. Lighthouse Service were merged to become the U.S. Coast Guard. The station shown here, built in 1903, no longer stands.. (*U.S. Coast Guard photo,* Lighthouse Digest *archives.*)

It's Brasswork, the Light-Keeper's Lament

By Frederic W. Morong, Jr.
1883-1947

After hearing numerous complaints from lighthouse keepers about the tedious chore of polishing all the brass at lighthouses, U.S. Lighthouse Service District Machinist Frederick W. Morong, Jr. sat down at the kitchen table at Little River Lighthouse in Cutler, Maine and wrote the poem. It's Brasswork, The Light-Keeper's Lament. *After the poem aired on a Boston radio station it gained national popularity with lighthouse keepers and was posted at many lighthouses nationwide. Morong eventually became a Lighthouse Engineer and later a Lighthouse Inspector.*

Oh what is the bane of a lightkeeper's life
That causes him worry, struggle and strife,
That makes him use cuss words and nag on his wife?
It's BRASSWORK

What makes him look ghastly consumptive and thin,
What robs him of health, vigor and vim,
And causes despair and drives him to sin?
It's BRASSWORK

The devil himself could never invent,
A material causing more world wide lament,
And in Uncle Sam's service about ninety percent
Is BRASSWORK

The lamp in the tower, reflector and shade,
The tools and accessories pass in the parade,
As a matter of fact the whole outfit is made
Of BRASSWORK

The oil containers I polish until
My poor back is broken, aching and still,
Each gallon, each quart, each pint and gill
Is BRASSWORK

I lay down to slumber all weary and sore,
I walk in my sleep, I awake with a snore,
And I'm shining the knob on my bedchamber door
That BRASSWORK

From pillar to post rags and polish I tote,
I'm never without them, for you will please note,
That even the buttons I wear on my coat,
Are BRASSWORK

The machinery, clockwork, and fog signal bell,
The coal hods, the dustpans, the pump in the well,
No I'll leave it to you mates...If this isn't...well,
BRASSWORK

I dig, scrub and polish, and work with a might,
And just when I get it all shining and bright,
In come the fog like a thief in the night,
Goodbye BRASSWORK

I start the next day when noontime draws near,
A boatload of summer visitors appear,
For no other reason than to smooch and besmear,
My BRASSWORK

So it goes along all summer, and along in the fall,
Comes the district machinists to overhaul,
and rub dirty paws all over,
My BRASSWORK

And again in the spring, if per chance it may be,
An efficiency star is awarded to me,
I open the package and what do I see?
More BRASSWORK

Oh, why should the spirit of mortal be proud,
In the short span of life that he is allowed,
If all the lining in every dark cloud,
Is BRASSWORK

And when I have polished until I am cold,
And I have taken my oath to the Heavenly fold,
Will my harp and my crown be made of pure gold?
No! BRASSWORK

About the Author

As one of the nation's leading lighthouse preservationists and historians, this is Harrison's tenth lighthouse book.

Harrison says his interest was inspired by a chance meeting many years ago with the late Ken Black, a retired Coast Guardsman, known by many as "Mr. Lighthouse," who founded the Shore Village Museum that later became the Maine Lighthouse Museum in Rockland, Maine. The museum now has the largest collection of lighthouse lenses, lighthouse artifacts and lighthouse memorabilia in the United States.

That chance meeting with Ken Black led Harrison to become the cofounder in 1992 of *Lighthouse Digest*, a lighthouse news and history magazine that grew from 34 original subscribers to a publication that now has world-wide circulation.

He is also the co-founder of Lighthouse Depot, "The World's Largest Lighthouse Gift Store," in Wells, Maine and the Lighthouse Depot Catalog, both of which he is now retired from.

In 1994 Harrison co-founded the non-profit New England Lighthouse Foundation that later became the American Lighthouse Foundation, where he served as president from 1994 to 2007. Harrison was also the primary creator of the American Lighthouse Foundation's Museum of Lighthouse History that in 2007 was merged into the Maine Lighthouse Museum in Rockland, Maine.

Although Harrison says he probably owns every lighthouse book ever printed, he rarely refers to another book when writing about a particular lighthouse. Having written hundreds of stories about lighthouses, he says he prefers to write stories from material derived from actual first hand memories, old documents, and other accounts written at the time. He has spent years researching lighthouses and locating old documents and photographs. However, as knowledgeable as he is about lighthouses, he does not consider himself a lighthouse expert, admitting that there are many others who he would put into that category.

Although Harrison now limits his speaking engagements, he has spoken to hundreds of audiences around the United States and Canada from crowds as large as 3,000 people to historical groups in small communities. He is sought after by the media as a resource person on lighthouse history and preservation, has been interviewed by numerous newspapers, radio stations, and television broadcasts and has been involved in a number of lighthouse film documentaries.

Harrison is also an original supporter of the annual Great Lakes Lighthouse Festival, held in Alpena, Michigan, and has donated artifacts from his personal collection to their museum.

Harrison has been the recipient of numerous awards from many organizations, including The Founders Award and the Presidents Award from the Outer Banks Lighthouse Society and the Great Lakes Lighthouse Award from the Great Lakes Lighthouse Festival. However, his most coveted honor was bestowed him in September of 2005, when Rear Admiral David Petoske, Commander of the First Coast Guard District, bestowed upon him the Homeland Security's United States Coast Guard's Meritorious Public Service Commendation Award and Medal for his direct involvement in numerous lighthouse preservation projects and the preserving of lighthouse history for future generations.

Today, Harrison continues with his busy activities as the editor and publisher of *Lighthouse Digest*; is on the Board of Directors of the American Lighthouse Foundation; is chairman of the Friends of Little River Lighthouse; is on the Board of Directors of the Maine Lighthouse Museum, editor of the *Lighthouse Depot Dispatch*, an e-mail newsletter, serves as co-chairman of his local church board; and he is working on several other lighthouse books.

Harrison has a true love for lighthouses and the preservation of their history, and a burning desire to save them for future generations. He says,

"One can learn more about early American history by researching and studying lighthouses than can be derived from any other single source." However, he has also stressed in lectures, presentations, and interviews that "It's important to remember that lighthouses were built for one purpose only: to save lives; now it's our turn to save the lighthouses. However, it is just as vitally important and, perhaps even more so, to save the photographs and memories of the lighthouse keepers and family members associated with the lighthouses, whether the structures are still standing or not. After all, without the people, the structures by themselves are meaningless."

To learn more about lighthouses,
you are invited to subscribe to

The Magazine of Lighthouses

P.O. Box 250
East Machias, ME 04630
(207) 259-2121
www.LighthouseDigest.net
Help Save the History

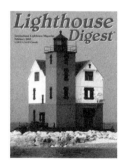

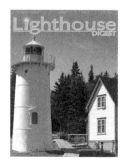

One can learn more about early American
History by studying lighthouses,
than from any other single source.

— Timothy Harrison —

Other books by Timothy E. Harrison

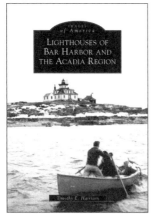

Lighthouses of Bar Harbor & the Acadia Region
(Maine)
$21.99

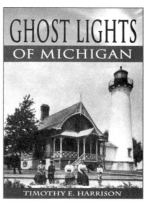

Ghost Lights of Michigan
$12.95

Portland Head Light,
A Pictorial Journey through Time
$16.95

Lighthouses of the Sunrise County
— Washington County Maine
$18.95

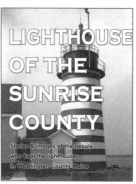

Lost Lighthouses
$17.95

Thunder Bay Island Lighthouse and Life Saving Station
$8.95

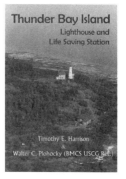

The Golden Age of American Lighthouses
$19.95

Lighthouse Digest
P.O. Box 250, East Machias, Maine 04630
(207)259-2121 — www.LighthouseDigest.net